D0759121

THE CHIEF EXECUTIVE OFFICERS

Books by Robert L. Shook

THE CHIEF EXECUTIVE OFFICERS

THE REAL ESTATE PEOPLE

THE ENTREPRENEURS

TEN GREATEST SALESPERSONS

WINNING IMAGES

THE COMPLETE PROFESSIONAL SALESMAN
(WITH Herbert Shook)

TOTAL COMMITMENT
(WITH Ronald Bingamen)

THE
CHIEF EXECUTIVE
OFFICERS

*Men Who Run Big Business
in America*

ROBERT L. SHOOK

1817

Harper & Row, Publishers, New York
Cambridge, Philadelphia, San Francisco,
London, Mexico City, São Paulo, Sydney

THE CHIEF EXECUTIVE OFFICERS. Copyright © 1981 by Robert L. Shook. All rights reserved. Printed in the United States of America. No part of this book may be used or reproduced in any manner whatsoever without written permission except in the case of brief quotations embodied in critical articles and reviews. For information address Harper & Row, Publishers, Inc., 10 East 53rd Street, New York, N.Y. 10022. Published simultaneously in Canada by Fitzhenry & Whiteside Limited, Toronto.

FIRST EDITION

Designer: Susan Hull

Library of Congress Cataloging in Publication Data

Shook, Robert L., 1938–
  The chief executive officers.
  1. Executives—United States—Interviews.   I. Title.
HF5500.3.U54S548   1981   658.4'09   81–47238
ISBN 0–06–014897–7   AACR2

81 82 83 84 85 10 9 8 7 6 5 4 3 2 1

To my son, R.J., with love

Acknowledgments

To Victor Barkman, Gladys Bowler, Harold Brown, Nancy Cone, William Corbett, C. Ramon Greenwood, Raymond Hayes, John Hoving, Jeanie Johnson, Robert Lazarus, Irv Levey, Steve Maloney, Tim McEnroe, Robert McCuen, Clifford Merriott, William Mullane, Jr., David Ostwald, Susan Piccione, Diane Rye, Jerome Schottenstein, Martin Shafiroff, Chuck Such, Laughran Vaber, Joseph Vecchione, and Phil Workman.

I am particularly grateful to Jeanne Desy, who helped me prepare my manuscript. And my most sincere gratitude to the ten CEOs I interviewed, who graciously volunteered their valuable time to share their philosophies, ideas, and stories.

Contents

THE CHIEF EXECUTIVE OFFICERS

Introduction

The influence of American business is enormous, reaching around the world and touching each of our lives. Of the more than 12 million businesses in the United States, a handful stand out as giants, each so large that in itself it is a significant factor in our society. Who are the men who run the giant corporations that play such an important role in our lives? They are not elected by the people, nor are their names and faces recognized by the average citizen. Even the few who have high public profiles are less well known than most athletes, entertainers, and politicians.

The fact that Americans show so little interest in the individuals who head our largest corporations is astonishing. Not one in a hundred people can name the CEOs of AT&T, Gulf, and General Electric—companies which greatly influence their daily lives. More amazing is the fact that many people cannot name the chief executive of the company they work for! In my opinion, that's equivalent to not knowing who is the governor of your state.

If Americans had blind faith in their business leaders, this lack of knowledge would be understandable. It would indicate that they had confidence in the system and believed the right people held the top positions. But this is far from the case.

Many Americans are anti–big business and mistrust business leaders as a group. Their "vote of no confidence" is a vote against the American tradition of free enterprise, an ideal which every American should cherish.

During my own years in business, I have come to feel more and more strongly that Americans need to know who the nation's foremost chief executives are. Since it isn't possible for each of us to meet personally with a top CEO, I decided to write about these executives. I knew that researching them would take time and gaining their consent for interviews would not be easy; no head of state follows a more hectic schedule than the CEOs of our nation's major corporations. Yet, they graciously volunteered their valuable time to participate in this book.

In selecting the companies I believed to be most influential, I chose not to simply use the ten largest corporations in America—a list which is top-heavy in the oil and automotive industries. Instead, I selected ten industries that have marked influence on American life. Once I had chosen an industry, I studied the chief executives of its major companies and chose one who could serve as a spokesman for his peers. Any short list is subject to debate; but I believe that, as a group, the individuals I interviewed are the elite of the business world. Let me introduce these ten CEOs to you in alphabetical order:

Robert A. Beck, Prudential Insurance Company of America, the largest insurance company in the world. Prudential insures over 50 million people.

Charles L. Brown, American Telephone and Telegraph Company, the largest *company* in the world. With assets in excess of $125 billion, AT&T employs over a million people.

Richard J. Ferris, UAL, Inc. United Airlines is America's largest airline.

Reginald H. Jones, General Electric Company. Perhaps the most innovative company in the world, GE holds more than 50,000 patents, far more than any other company.

Ralph Lazarus, Federated Department Stores, the nation's

largest operator of department stores, with 1980 net sales of $6.3 billion.

Jerry McAfee, Gulf Oil Corporation. In 1980, Gulf had revenues of nearly $29 billion.

David W. Mitchell, Avon Products, Inc., the world's largest manufacturer and distributor of cosmetics, fragrances, and costume jewelry, with more than 1.2 million representatives selling its products.

Thomas A. Murphy, General Motors Corporation, the largest manufacturing company in the world. GM employs approximately 850,000 people.

James D. Robinson III, American Express Company, a worldwide diversified financial institution. The American Express card is honored in more than 150 countries.

Irving S. Shapiro, the Du Pont Company. With 1980 sales of $13.7 billion, Du Pont is the largest chemical company in the world.

The diverse products these companies deal with include insurance, air travel, oil, electrical apparatus, retail goods, cosmetics, automobiles, financial and travel services, and chemicals. The companies are clearly leaders in their respective industries. Similarly, the CEOs themselves are leaders among their peers. In a 1980 *Wall Street Journal*/Gallup survey, 306 chief executive officers of large corporations were asked to name the most respected business leaders in the United States. In order, their top three choices were GE's Reginald Jones, Du Pont's Irving Shapiro, and GM's Thomas Murphy—all included in this book.

The Chief Executive Officers noticeably lacks a chapter on a woman or black CEO. As you read the book, you will realize that the depth of experience and judgment demanded of a CEO usually requires decades of work in the industry. Unfortunately, few women or blacks have had the opportunity to enter corporate management until recently. It is my firm belief, however, that a book written about the leading CEOs of 1990 will include the minorities which have heretofore been excluded—not by business alone but by our society in general.

It is likely that one or more of the chief executives included here will retire either before or shortly after the publication of this book. In light of the vast experience required of those who hold top positions, the CEOs of most large corporations are in their sixties when they assume the positions. Therefore, the mathematical probability is that at least one in ten CEOs will reach mandatory retirement age every year. However, one of the primary functions of a CEO is management development and long-term planning for his company. Long after he is gone, his impact will be felt. The decisions made by today's chief executive are very likely to influence the lives of our grandchildren in the twenty-first century.

My research and observations during my interviews with the CEOs confirmed that these are people of the highest integrity, whose dedication to their communities and their nation is very real. Their activities and the philosophies they share in these chapters strongly support this conclusion. Unfortunately, our media are often guilty of reporting only "sensational" news about business leaders. Similarly, newspapers are eager to report a stick-up on Main Street, but don't print a story about a woman on Elm Street who takes time to bake an apple pie for a new neighbor. While only a fraction of 1 percent of all businessmen may be found guilty of wrongdoing, the public is given those stories in blazing headlines. The other side of the story—corporate and individual responsibility and philanthropy—goes unreported. As a consequence, the average American forms a one-sided picture of modern business leaders and of their companies.

It is popular today to think of corporations as having no souls. This is not a new notion. Over a hundred years ago, Henry David Thoreau addressed the question: "It is true enough that a corporation has no conscience; but a corporation of conscientious men is a corporation with a conscience." This book spotlights the conscientious men who help form the consciences of the corporations they lead.

It is also popular to believe that "bigness is bad"—that a big corporation is necessarily a worse thing to have around than ten little companies would be. But I believe the free enterprise system actually guarantees that only good companies will grow. When there is competition for the consumer's dollar, only the best individuals and companies survive. Eventually, the business which does the best job is the most successful. Our large corporations all began as small companies, and grew because they performed brilliantly. It is unfair to chastise them for their success by assuming that bigness is bad. As a matter of fact, a good argument can be made for the other side— the giant corporations are big because they offer value. In other words, "bigness is good." At the very least, we should keep our minds open in considering any company, and not judge its integrity solely on its size.

An understanding of the place of a giant corporation is more valuable now than ever in our history. Every one of us depends on goods and services which could not be supplied by small companies. Imagine a nation with a thousand little phone systems! Or consider whether such a thing as a small automobile manufacturer is even possible. How about a small airline or a small railroad? The fact is that the very nature of many products and services we consider essential to our affluent life-style demands that large companies produce them. Certain businesses, if they exist at all, must be large. In the twentieth century, a nation of only small shopkeepers could not survive.

If we really consider the place of major corporations in American life, we are likely to reach the conclusion that our major corporations are one of our most important "natural resources." They have made considerable contributions to this nation, and are directly responsible for the fact that Americans have the highest standard of living in the world. Corporations are major employers, and in fact, many communities eagerly offer inducements to companies looking for new plant locations. These communities know that the giant company not only brings in jobs, but actively encourages community and civic work and often gives generous support to cultural activities. Moreover, as individuals and as a nation, we need the products corporations supply us with. If any one big industry—say, automotive—simply disappeared overnight, the United States would immediately fall to the status of a third-rate industrial nation.

Many people have expressed surprise that the CEOs of these large corporations were willing to take the time for interviews, and to share the stories of their careers. "They do it to feed their egos," one cynic told me. I don't deny that these men, like all achievers, have healthy egos; I do maintain that there is a great difference between a healthy ego and an egotistical need for recognition. I choose to believe that these ten executives participated in this book because they had something important to say. To a man, they believe deeply in America, and in the free enterprise system. Their commitment to American business is evidenced in their biosketches, which show the organizations they support and the leadership roles they play. They are telling their stories because they wish to share their successes and philosophies with their fellow Americans.

The stories of these CEOs also emphasize that the American Dream is alive and flourishing. Time and again, their chapters illustrate how an individual can start at a lower level of a multinational corporation and rise to the top position. Tom Murphy began at General Motors as a clerk in the Accounting Department. Dave Mitchell went to work for Avon as a mail boy after he graduated from high school. Bob Beck started his career with Prudential as an insurance salesman. Charlie Brown first worked for AT&T during his college summer vacations as a ditch digger with a crew putting up telephone poles. Their success indicates that opportunities are still abundant in the corporate world. As they will affirm, there is a constant search for individuals with talent, who possess a total commitment to their work.

Join me in meeting ten of the finest men in our society—
The Chief Executive Officers: Men Who Run Big Business in America.

1

Robert A. Beck

CHAIRMAN OF THE BOARD
AND CHIEF EXECUTIVE OFFICER,
THE PRUDENTIAL INSURANCE COMPANY OF
AMERICA

Prior to joining Prudential as a full-time agent in 1951, Bob Beck served as a financial analyst with the Ford Motor Company in Detroit for about one year. In 1956, he became a manager for Prudential's Cincinnati agency. Subsequently he served as director of agencies in the South Central home office in Jacksonville, Florida, a position he held from 1957 to 1963. In 1963, he became the executive general manager at Prudential's corporate office in Newark, New Jersey. Bob was elected vice president in 1965, and the following year became senior vice president in charge of the Mid-America home office in Chicago. In 1967, he became senior vice president in charge of the Corporate Office Ordinary Agencies Department. From 1970 to 1974, he served as executive vice president in charge of marketing. He became the company's twelfth president in 1974. Four years later, at the relatively young age of fifty-three, he was elected chairman of the board and chief executive officer.

An alumnus of Fordham University, Bob graduated summa cum laude from Syracuse University in 1950. He received the chartered life underwriter designation from the American College in 1954 and the college's diploma in agency management in 1961.

Presently, Bob is a director of Campbell Soup Company and Xerox Corporation. He is a trustee of Syracuse University and the Committee for Economic Development, as well as a member of the Conference Board and the Business Council. A member of the Business Roundtable, he is also chairman of the group's Task Force on Social Security, and serves on its Policy Committee. He is a member of the Advisory Council of the Columbia University Graduate School of Business, and a board member and past president of the New Jersey Historical Society. He is vice chairman and immediate past chairman of the Greater Newark Chamber of Commerce. He is also immediate past chairman of the Garden State Bowl Committee as well as the Silver Anniversary Committee of the Independent College Fund of New Jersey. He is a board member of the New Jersey State Chamber of Commerce and the United Way of America, and chairman of the United Way's Long-Range Planning Committee.

A board member of the American Council of Life Insurance, Bob also serves on the ACLI's Executive Roundtable Committee. He is past chairman of the Health Insurance Association of America and of the Life Insurance Marketing and Research Association. He is a board member of the American College and chairman of the college's Capital Gifts Committee. He serves as the insurance industry's co-chairman for the United Negro College Fund Capital Resources Development Program, and he is a Knight of Malta.

Bob was born on October 6, 1925, in New York City. He and his wife, Frances, live in Rumson, New Jersey. They have five children: Robert II, Arthur, Stephen, Kathleen, and Teresa.

The size of the Prudential Insurance Company of America, the largest insurance company in the world, is mind-boggling. The company insures over 50 million people and employs more than 24,000 agents throughout the United States and Canada. On December 31, 1980, Prudential's life insurance in force totaled over $406 billion. With assets of $59.8 billion, the company invested an average of $24 million each working day.

Prudential's continuing growth is equally astounding. In 1980, for instance, total life insurance in force increased $39 billion. The company's assets increased $5.1 billion. Only a handful of the nation's more than 1,700 insurance companies have achieved equivalent production *in their entire history!* To an outsider, the sheer size of this great insurer/financial institution can be overwhelming. Yet to its associates, the company is affectionately and simply known as "Pru."

Meeting Bob Beck quickly dispels any notions that financial empires of this size are still headed by the likes of the overbearing J. P. Morgan. Prudential's CEO is relaxed and unassuming. The office of chairman has obviously not changed him a bit. His down-to-earth attitude is perhaps epitomized by the varnished, plated Army Pickmatic that sits on a small conference table in a corner of his office. He takes it up and explains,

ROBERT A. BECK

"My father gave this to me many years ago, and it tells me an important message: 'If you can't find a way, make one.' These were just common entrenching tools used by foot soldiers to dig foxholes and trenches. I like having this here. It reminds me that every problem has a solution. It may take some digging, but there's a solution."

Bob remembers with fondness his own five years in the service. Although he has never worked for any insurance company but Prudential, the roots of his insurance career lie in his military experience. As a parachute infantry officer in the 82nd Airborne Division during World War II, he hurt his ankle on a jump. When he was released from the hospital, he was not allowed to go back to regular full-time duty because of the injury; instead, he was given the job of division education officer. "I'd only been there a while," he recalls, "when I decided that they really needed to do something about their National Service Life Insurance. So I asked the chief of staff to make me the insurance officer as well. I became very involved in getting people in the Eighty-second to sign up for NSLI, and that's when I got to know a Prudential agent on post. He thought I ought to become an agent, and kept insisting that I should sell insurance part time when I left the service and went back to college. He was so determined that the morning I was to leave the post to muster out, he woke me up at seven to give me a letter of introduction to a marketing vice president of the Prudential.

"Well, truthfully, I didn't intend to follow up on it, but my wife insisted I at least meet with Pat MacLeod, the Prudential vice president mentioned in the letter. I did it more out of courtesy than anything else." Bob smiles. "He charmed the devil out of me, and I decided to sell insurance while I went to school."

Intending to make his career in insurance, Bob majored in marketing and insurance at the University of Syracuse. However, upon graduating, he accepted a position as financial analyst with the Ford Motor Company in Detroit. "It was a super experience," he declares enthusiastically. "I was with the brightest, sharpest people I'd ever met. There were about sixty of us in a group that had become known as the 'Whiz Kids.' Robert McNamara was Ford's comptroller at the time, and the group was full of Phi Beta Kappas and Beta Gamma Sigmas. All but two of us had been to graduate school, and some had worked on their doctorates. I really enjoyed working with those people, but it just wasn't for me. I felt too far removed from the action, and after eight months I resigned.

"The idea of selling insurance still appealed to me," he continues. "Since I knew people in Syracuse, I called the Prudential manager there and said I'd like to be associated with that particular agency. Then Frances and I took our forty-six dollars out of the bank, borrowed five hundred, and drove nineteen hours through the blizzard of 1951 from Detroit to Syracuse."

Looking a little sheepish, he adds, "At the time I actually didn't realize I had to apply for the job. I thought because I had sold for Prudential in college I was automatically in. So when I talked to the manager, I wasn't aware that when he told me to 'come on along to Syracuse,' he wasn't actually giving me a job. As a matter of fact, he had sent me a letter suggesting that I visit his office so they could take a look at me and I could take a look at them. 'Then we'll decide,' the letter said, 'whether you should become associated with the agency.' That letter was en route to my Detroit address while I was driving through the blizzard. It's probably a good thing I didn't receive it. I might have had second thoughts if I had."

Bob's chief reason for choosing Prudential was that he liked the people with the company he had previously known. "It was a first-class operation run by good people, and everybody associated with Pru was well motivated. The company was said to be the best in the business, and from what I had seen, it lived up to that reputation. And I had learned in my military days that I liked being with the leader."

Like most agents, Bob was approached from time to time during his career by other insurance companies that wanted him to become associated with them. "If you're a decent producer," he says with a shrug, "there are always plenty of people knocking on the door. But every time I considered making a change, I began to think about the strength of Pru's people and all the friendships I had made. Then I thought about my confidence in the company and our products, and most important, what the company actually stood for. And, well, I never found a good reason to seriously consider another company."

There was, however, a time when Bob considered leaving the insurance business altogether. When he had been a full-time agent for about nine months, he hit a slump. "Now, slumps are not unusual," he says quickly. "Almost every sales-person has them—a few days without a sale, even a week. We have a sort of rule of thumb. If you go without a sale a full week, that's trouble. If you go two weeks, it's really getting bad. Three weeks, and it's very serious indeed. If you go five weeks, it's reconstruction time, because after five weeks you've lived with defeat so long you're probably beyond resurrection. Well, I went *eight* weeks."

He shakes his head. "I can smile about it now," he says, "but nobody was smiling then. It got to the point that if I were going out for an evening appointment and I saw a light in a window on the left side of the house, I'd turn around and head home because it was a bad omen! Obviously, they weren't going to buy. I can remember coming home and taking my dinner to the bedroom to eat because I couldn't face my wife any more. I was really in the depths of despair. I can't recall ever being so badly shaken. Up until that time, everything had gone pretty well for me. People had always predicted that I would be successful at whatever I did. But now I was proving their belief in me to be wrong.

"Then one night I went up to the top of a high hill behind Le Moyne College, and I sat there for several hours and talked to myself. I began to reconstruct my whole life. To this day, I don't know exactly what happened up on that hill, but when I came down, I was a new person. On my next twenty inter-views, I made seventeen sales. I had the feeling that prospects just couldn't say no to me. Naturally, it boils down to having the right attitude. My prospects weren't any better than the ones I had called on during my eight-week slump. And I didn't have any more knowledge. It was just a whole new attitude."

Bob leans back in his chair and comments, "Of all the personal experiences I've had in this business, none has served me better than that one. Because every time I worked with a struggling agent, I knew what it was like to be frustrated, lacking in confidence, totally shaken." Past and present Prudential agents verify that Bob has an unusual ability to identify with agents—those who are having trouble as well as the superstars. "You know *he's been there,*" one agent says. "He's not isolated in an ivory tower like some senior executives. He has a feel for what's happening out in the field."

Bob recalls a sales experience shortly after his eight-week slump that demonstrates the change in his attitude. "One evening, I called on my seven o'clock appointment, and when I knocked on the door the man's wife answered. I introduced myself and explained that I was there to see her husband, but I was very happy to have the two of them present, since life insurance also involved her welfare. She went off to tell him I was there.

"She left the door ajar, so I could hear the conversation. 'The Prudential agent is here. He says you have an appointment.'

" 'Oh, doggone it!' (Actually, he expressed himself rather more strongly than that.) 'Tell him to go away.'

" 'I already told him you were home. I can't do that. He's standing at the door now.'

" 'Oh, nuts,' he said. 'Well, let him in, and we'll get rid of him in a hurry so we can still catch the movie.'

"Now, during my slump," Bob continues, "if I'd heard a conversation like that, I would have disappeared by the time she got back to the door. But my attitude was different now, and I hung in there. To make a long story short, at twelve-thirty that night we were having coffee and cake, and I walked out with an application and a check. As I said, it's all in the mind. Every new salesman has to learn that. That man wasn't saying no to me. He was saying no to a situation that threatened him with the need to make a decision, that would cause him to spend money he would have liked to have a bit more freedom to spend elsewhere."

Laying his unlit cigar in an ashtray, Bob smiles. "I remember another interesting sale during my early days in the business. I had called on a sixty-four-year-old man who was publishing a Polish newspaper. He needed extra life insurance, and I convinced him to buy it. But because he had high blood pressure and was overweight, a rated policy was issued. He didn't have a firm understanding about how insurance worked, so he wanted me to cut the price for him. He kept pouring me glass after glass of his Polish liqueur; I believe he thought that if I got drunk I'd soften up and give him a better rate. Well, he kept working on me, and I kept working on him.

"Finally I told him, 'Look, this is a contract that's going to last for fourteen years. After fourteen years, if you're still alive, you're going to get back every dime you put into this plan except for the last year's premium. Now, if you die before that time, your beneficiary gets back *more* than you put in. If you could know right now that you were going to live for the next fourteen years, you'd be thrilled to pay for it with just one year's premium, wouldn't you?' He nodded, and I knew the sale was made. 'Okay, that's enough conversation. Just make out your check to Prudential.' With that, I kept quiet, and he stared at me for a moment, got up, and started writing out his check!

"That's the only time I had someone seriously try to horse-trade," Bob says with a chuckle. "Actually, I dislike that kind of dickering very much, which is one of the reasons I chose insurance—I like the fact that the price of a policy is predetermined. It's not a business where you bargain and horsetrade the way you do when you buy a car. In fact, to show you how much I dislike that kind of thing, about ten years ago I went to see a local car dealer, and I told him, 'I don't like shopping around for a new car. I like to find a dealer I can trust, who will give me a fair price. So I don't want to barter with you. Just give me a price, and I'll take it or leave it. There will be no dickering, and I won't waste a lot of time. All I want is a fair price, and if I feel that you're not taking advantage of me, I'll buy all my cars from you.'

"Well, this dealer has treated me fairly, and I've bought all our cars from him this way ever since. I don't even ask the price until it's delivered. There's never any horsetrading. This is what I liked so much about the insurance business," Bob repeats. "Everyone in a given age bracket with good health who buys the same life insurance policy will get the same rate. So instead of having to worry about bartering, an agent can concentrate on the product and on giving his customers good service.

"I also liked insurance because I wanted to sell a product I could take pride in, one I believed was honestly valuable. I never had to apologize for my product, and this, I think, is important. Again, it gets back to attitude. People can sense how you really feel about your product, so the enthusiasm you have for it is a major factor in determining your success. That's why it was so important for me to really believe in my product and my company. And I always have."

Bob worked as an agent and assistant manager in Syracuse from February 1951 until November 1953, and then moved to Newark as a training consultant. In February 1955, he relocated to Jacksonville as a regional supervisor and assistant director of agencies. The next year, he became an agency manager in Cincinnati. "I decided to seek a career in management," he explains, "because I was very excited about working with people. I was a good producer as an agent, but I wasn't a world beater. And I discovered that it wasn't as easy for me to do what I needed to do for myself as it was for me to direct other people. I really liked training people. I thrived on helping them develop and become successful. And I suppose I simply enjoyed the function of being responsible, too."

A career insurance person can choose one of three general paths: sales, field management, or home office management.

All three paths, Bob thinks, can be equally rewarding financially. "You have to pick the track most fulfilling to you. Now, I personally didn't feel that sales production offered the excitement and romance I was looking for. I got that from working with people. When I first went into management, I hired nine agents within fourteen months, and every one of them became successful. Yet each of these nine agents was completely different. It was such a thrill to be able to work with completely different individuals who all had different styles. And I was able to do things for them I wouldn't have done for myself. I knew those methods weren't necessarily good for me, but they worked for these individuals. I can't tell you the satisfaction it gave me. So I quickly discovered that my strong suit was working with others."

Much of Bob's success in management is often credited to his tell-it-as-it-is approach. He is quick to point out that the insurance business is not for everyone, and he never pulled his punches in recruiting prospective agents. "I'm a big believer in telling the problems as well as the good points," he says. "Too many young men and women come into this business without knowing the hurdles they'll have to face. When I was in field management, I'd tell applicants, 'If you're right for this business, the problems are opportunities. If you're not right for this business, it can be pretty rough out there. There are a great many people who really can't survive in a world that's other than nine to five. They need a structured job. By the same token, some people need a salary. They're not happy if they don't know how much they're going to receive at the end of the week.'

"Now, on the other hand," Bob continues, "I would tell them that there are those who want to work on a straight commission. They feel this is the only way to get paid what they're really worth. They don't want to be strongly structured; they want the freedom to grow and develop as fast as they have the capacity to do it. They want to accept the full responsibility for their own performance. And for people like this, the insurance business is a big plus."

One can sense how much enjoyment Bob obtained from working with agents when he describes how he would recruit new agents. "I was a tough supervisor," he says, "and I never tried to conceal that fact. I'd tell a prospective agent, 'If you're willing to come into the agency with me on my terms, you'll be successful. Now we're going to set up a make-believe corporation, and you and your wife will own about 10 percent of the voting stock. I'm going to own 90 percent. But you're going to take in all the profits, and you're going to buy back some of that voting stock from me on the basis of your performance, your skills, and your productivity. Until you get really good, however, I'm still going to own most of the voting stock. Even when you become a superior producer, I'll still own 30 to 40 percent of the voting stock, because that's my responsibility to you.

" 'Now, if you want someone who's going to be easier on you, who will be tolerant when you do things wrong, who won't compel you to do the things you must do in order to be successful, then you're better off going with somebody else. In fact, I can give you the names of some people who will accept that. But if you want to come into an agency where you cannot fail, then you come with me.' " A big smile flashes on Bob's face as he adds, "And let me tell you, I got anybody who was good! And I needed good agents, because I expected a lot from them. I always felt that my job was to develop each agent so he could use his strengths most effectively, and I put a lot into that. If an agent wavered, I was on his back until he was straightened out."

To see the confident CEO of Prudential now, it's hard to believe that Bob Beck went through the typical struggles of a young agent. But he is the first to confess that he did. "I could always sympathize with new agents," he reminisces, "because I can remember the struggle I'd had with my attitude in the early days. When I'd get up to face that big world out there, I'd have to stand in front of the mirror and give myself a pep talk: 'You're going to have a good day, Bob. This is going to be a really positive day, and you're going to make a lot of sales.' Of course, the first sale I had to make was that sale I was making to myself in the mirror! So I'd give myself the pitch and then I'd start to hum and sing and force myself to feel good. Before very long, it got to be a habit. I would wake up feeling enthusiastic. I didn't have to work at it nearly as often. Feeling good became part of my style. I believe anyone can do the same thing—learn the habit of feeling good.

"You have to like what you do," he adds. "If you don't, you'll tend to evade your responsibilities, or at least not perform your functions very well. Every job has some aspects that are hard to like. I recall one position I had that called for serving as master of ceremonies at our recognition dinners. Well, I enjoyed making a major presentation or talk, but I didn't enjoy introducing people. Then one night on my way to a dinner, I thought about it. I realized that my attitude was stupid. I was going to have to do this quite a bit, possibly for the rest of my life, so I might as well start enjoying it. Besides, if I really worked hard at it, I *could* enjoy it. And I did. That evening I had a super time. And from then on, I always enjoyed being MC. If you have to do it, why not enjoy it?"

A summa cum laude graduate of Syracuse, Bob cites the insurance industry's commitment to professionalism as one of its attractions for him. "I'm a student. I love to learn. This industry requires that an individual make a commitment to a lifetime of learning, and that aspect had great appeal to me. Quite frankly, I would become bored in a business that didn't require constant growth and change. And believe me, the marketplace has changed so much since I entered this field that if I hadn't continued to grow, the business would have walked away from me.

"This business requires that I continually strive to be the best at my trade, and that's what I love so much about it. I can match my skills and desire to excel with those of the best people in the field. Of course, much of anyone's success depends on a willingness to pay the price. Assuming you have reasonable intelligence, that willingness is the number one requirement. If you have it, the sky's the limit. And I wanted to be in a business where my advancement was unlimited. I'm five eleven and I weigh 180 pounds. I wouldn't want to be out on the football field or the basketball courts with guys six two to six ten who weigh 250 pounds, because nothing I could ever do would permit me to compete with them effectively. In my career, I want to have equal footing, or more than equal footing if I can get it. And in this industry, I knew I could aim at the sky."

Even early in his career, Bob had big ambitions. "In fact," he admits, "it entered my mind very early on that I would like to be CEO of Prudential. Now, that's the kind of thing people are sometimes reluctant to say. However, I used to say it when I was young and new in the business. Then I stopped saying it. But enough people remember me saying that was my goal that it's a matter of public record, so I guess that's something I can't disavow now."

Frances, Bob's wife of thirty-two years, always shared his ambition. "When we grew up," she says, "we still believed in dreams, we still believed in fairy tales. We shared the dream that Bob would someday head the world's foremost insurance company, and we worked together at it for all these years."

Bob concurs. "I think you have to have great dreams, big dreams—that's what living is all about. Even if you don't make it, and there are times when everybody has doubts, a great deal of the joy of life is reaching out for one's dreams. In fact, it's often anticlimactic to get there. Then you have to find another goal to substitute for the one you've reached. That leads to a lot of quiet reflection in your room late at night when you try to figure out what you've done and what you want to aim for next. And as a CEO I have the opportunity to dream not just for myself but for the organization I'm involved in. Where is it going to go? How is it going to get there? If I have an idea, how fast do I try to sell it to the organization? How much should I reveal of what I want to do? Do I risk letting others know what I'm trying to do too soon and losing their confidence? Do I risk waiting too long? That's what makes all the wheels turn."

One of the reasons Bob has met his big ambitions has been the enthusiasm and dedication he brought to every position he held at Prudential. "I've always liked each job," he says, "and I've always believed a person should work at each job as though he's going to be there for the rest of his life, even though he may be planning to move beyond that position in the future. When someone taps you on the shoulder and says, 'We'd like to promote you,' you must always be ready. But you can't fake it. If you try to make a quick, splashy performance and they don't happen to tap you at the right time, the operation can be falling apart by the time a vacancy does occur, and you'll no longer be considered a candidate. You have to work at every job as though you'll always be there. Then you'll never need to apologize for the results."

Although Bob has enjoyed his entire career, he admits to eventually becoming somewhat bored when he was director of agencies in Jacksonville from 1957 to 1963. "I loved the people I was working with," he stresses, "but it was the kind of work that in order to do well I had to repeat the same things day in and day out. My work with agencies required me to periodically review their plans, supervise their development, help with the selection of new agents, and assist in the promotion of sales growth. So I was continually going over a checklist in order to see that the job was being properly done. That responsibility was exciting and challenging for the first four or five years, but after a while, well, it got to be old hat. Sure, there was still some challenge, but the job had begun to lose its excitement for me. That's when I started writing a book about attitude, because I needed an outside activity. But I was transferred to the position of executive general manager in the corporate headquarters, so I've never had the opportunity to finish the book. The outline is still intact, and one day I'll write my book."

At Prudential, Bob is considered a driving, dynamic executive—one with a voracious appetite for work, who makes hard, practical decisions. Few people who have known him during his thirty years with Prudential would characterize him as a dreamer. But the dreams have always been there. And the achievement has always followed. With a delighted grin and a gleam in his eyes, he says, "I love my job. There's not another job anywhere I'd rather have.

"I think it's a shame that so many people live and die with the music still in them. I find very few people who really get anywhere close to working at their potential. And the major reason for it is that they are not really motivated. They put in time rather than use it. We spend so much of our time working, why not have fun at it? Why not feel the thrill of getting something done, of winning, of being in front of the pack? That's what makes the day feel good."

Bob's own day starts at six with a vitamin pill and some juice. Then he takes a cup of coffee and three packed briefcases to his car. While driver Maurice O'Shea takes him the fifty-five miles from his home in Rumson, New Jersey, to corporate headquarters in Newark, Bob puts in the first seventy or eighty minutes of his working day. His company-owned green Ford LTD has been described as a mobile office; it contains a desk made of Lucite with one side anchored into a fitting on the door and the other resting on the back seat. The backs of the two front seats hold pouches, one "For File," and the other "For Action." The pouches come equipped with routing slips, paper clips, stapler, and other office paraphernalia. A tensor light extends over the back of the front seat. Although the car is equipped with a telephone, Bob avoids spending much time making calls. "I'm just as productive in my car as in the office," he explains. "Maybe more so, because there are no interruptions. So I guard that time very jealously. I concentrate completely on what I'm doing. I'm not even aware of the motion of the car. My driver might comment as I'm getting out, 'Gee, that was a terrible accident,' and I'll look at him and say, 'What accident?' "

When Bob arrives at his office, the "For File" materials

go in one direction, and the "For Action" materials go to his office. For the first half hour or so of the day, he gives his secretary, Diane Rye, just about everything he will give her that day. Then there may be time for one or two phone calls before his first meeting at nine. From then until it's time to go home he is booked with meetings, some on a one-to-one basis, and some with several other people. The Executive Office, for instance, consists of Bob, the president, and four executive vice presidents, and meets about a hundred times a year for an average of three hours per meeting. Further meetings are scheduled for lunch in the Prudential dining room. So full is Bob's calendar that it is likely to be two or three months in the future before he has an open lunch date. When he leaves the office at six or six-thirty, he continues to work in the car until he gets home. Dinner with the family lasts about an hour, and then Bob retreats to his study, where he works from eight-thirty until about midnight.

With this schedule, Bob tries to preserve weekends for the family; nevertheless, about one-fourth of his weekend days are devoted to business commitments. Bob usually spends Friday evening, Saturday, and Sunday morning and afternoon with the family. Sunday after dinner he again goes to his study to begin the next work week. "A lot of people think senior executives are figureheads," he says, "jet setters who really don't work very hard. Well, I don't see that kind of thing among the senior executives I know. They couldn't survive if they weren't constantly reading and studying. They wouldn't understand anything that's going on in their business. Take the changing marketplace. If you stayed out of the reading files for just a couple of months, you'd be lost. It takes a total commitment to keep on top of things."

Averaging about five hours of sleep a night, Bob nevertheless maintains a steady high level of energy. He attributes this to his enthusiasm for his work. "Being motivated and positive is certainly part of it," he says. "And I don't think that's something you're born with. The ability to maintain a zestful, positive attitude is something you learn. But I don't believe

I'm unusually energetic. Really, a high energy level is vital for any senior executive."

It is typical of Bob that he has done what he can to minimize the strain of the working day. To the right of his nine-foot desk is an unusual apparatus, a custom-made drawing board–desk, positioned so he can work at it standing. A second telephone is built into the wall here. "I work here all the time," he explains, "except when I'm attending meetings. I'd rather be standing than sitting. It prevents back strain, and it's good exercise. Much of my personal writing is done at my stand-up desk."

His "sit-down" desk is designed so that four people can sit around it informally with the same leverage; thus he can conduct small conferences at it without somebody looking over somebody else's shoulder. The spacious office also holds fourteen built-in hanging file drawers along the wall behind his desk and a large library of reference books. It is an office to work in. "I've got a pet peeve about non-functional furniture in offices," he admits. A quick glance around confirms this. Although furnished tastefully, his office is streamlined and functional.

Obviously, Bob is a man who likes to put 100 percent of himself into everything he does, work or play. During his leisure time, he crams in as many activities as possible. His first love is fishing, and when the weather permits, he and Frances can be found on their twenty-four-foot 115-horsepower outboard. Scuba diving is another favorite sport; Bob reminisces about diving with actor Lloyd Bridges in Hawaii several years ago. He likes golf, too, and comments, "Even if you're not an expert, the handicap system permits you to compete with the top players." He also plays paddle tennis and squash, and if these sports aren't available, he'll jog. He also enjoys indoor games, such as bridge and backgammon. A few years ago he even tried hang gliding, but had to give it up when Pru's chief actuary refused to issue him additional life insurance unless he quit! Once Bob took a look at the statistics, he was convinced.

The Becks both enjoy a night out dancing and love just being together and "having a good time." They get involved socially only on Friday and Saturday nights; weekday evenings are reserved for work at home or business activities. Frances and Bob do get away on three or four short vacations a year, for a total of around thirty days. And, although Bob delegates authority and responsibility to other executives during these trips, he can always be reached while on vacation if he's really needed.

As one of the duties of his office, Bob speaks to many audiences during the year, and a question women often ask is "Do you think the price you and your family pay for you to be chairman is worth it?" Bob replies, "Well, there are obviously many people who don't think so, because they don't pay it. But my wife and I feel very good about it. We made a decision in the beginning that this was what we wanted, and we are very comfortable with the kind of life we lead." He also points out the importance of this kind of agreement within the family. "I've always been impressed with the high quality of the senior executives I've met," he says, "not only at Pru but also at other companies. But I'm equally impressed with their wives and how they relate to their husbands. There's no question that it takes a team effort. Without the support of your spouse, this job would be very, very difficult."

Bob was transferred fourteen times during the first twenty years of the Becks' marriage, and there's no question that Frances has become an expert in moving. "The secret to packing," she says, "is making sure that you have the beds, bedding, and towels coming off the moving van first. Once you set up sleeping arrangements and the bathrooms, the rest is easy." She remembers only one bad experience during the family's many relocations. "We once bought a house in Chicago, at least we thought we did. Working from a floor plan, I packed everything and labeled each piece of furniture for its position in the house. Then the deal fell through. It meant unpacking, deciding which pieces to take to a house rented at the last minute, and what had to be stored. It was a lot of extra work, but everything worked out."

"She's a super partner," Bob says, smiling. "Sure, there were a few times in the early days when she fussed about the hours I was putting in. So I'd say, 'Okay, honey, I'll give up this commission work and get a nine-to-five job somewhere. Of course, we'll have to get rid of your car, and we may have to sell the china and silver, and I guess we might as well forget about those elaborate schools for the kids.' After a few minutes we'd both laugh, and that would be the end of it. We've never had a serious argument about my career. It got so I'd come home and say, 'Guess what?' and she'd know we were being transferred again. That became our way of communicating. She'd answer, 'Okay, where are we going?'

"This question of transfers as people work their way up through a company is becoming more difficult," Bob points out. "Now that both partners in a marriage are very often developing their own careers and sinking their own roots, it's a growing issue. Developing young executives today requires a lot of care and sympathetic understanding on the part of management. In our case, since Frances wasn't working outside the home, we didn't have that problem."

Bob readily admits that the husband-wife team effort has been a major factor in his success. While he manages Prudential's $54 billion in assets, Frances balances the family budget. She's also the one more intimately involved in local church, civic, and charitable activities. Then, too, she has taken a great deal of the day-to-day responsibility for raising their five children. "I'm sure the children have had to make some sacrifices," Bob says. "Our oldest son, Bob, had attended fourteen schools by the time he got to college. And I have not always had the time with them I would have liked. But I believe that the quality of the time spent with children is more important than the quantity. I always try to spend time with each of them individually, although admittedly it's not a great deal of time."

At present, Bob is tutoring his daughter Teresa from nine

to nine-thirty most evenings when he's home. He enjoys this chance to be with her. "She's having trouble with a badly written economics text," he explains, "so she'll come in and ask for my help, and I'm really thrilled that she wants me to give her a hand. She's a good, solid, dependable student, so it's not very often I get a chance to help her with a school problem.

"We're very proud of our children," he continues. "Each of them marches to a different drummer, of course, but they're all doing a super job. Naturally, one may take longer than another to find his or her own way, but there's no big rush. Our youngest son, Stephen, wasn't too excited about school, for instance, so he joined the Army recently after two years of college. Stephen is an outgoing, involved, and interested person who really wants to make things happen. The military experience will give him the balance he needs for the future. I strongly support his decision. My father was a career military man, and my Army years were a great learning experience for me. It was my experience in the military that taught me how much I liked working with people. The Army is great training for young people. They give you an assignment which you may know nothing about, and they expect you to do it anyway. Pretty soon you learn that you can do almost anything you want to once you decide the job has to be done.

"Our son Arthur has been in and out of college and has worked between terms and during the school year." Bob is also supportive of this decision. "So what if an individual is somewhat older than the average student when he or she graduates?" he says. "What's important, I believe, is that young people get the right values, and then in the long run they'll get more out of their education than most. Arthur has grown and developed into a unique individual with great social mobility. I think he'll be successful at whatever he chooses for his life's work.

"Our daughter Kathleen is a student at the American Academy of Dramatic Arts in New York City. She is a real competitor. At one point she was actively interested in forensics. From the second meet on, she always finished first in all the competitions she engaged in. Kathleen's love for dramatics led her to the American Academy. She is very happy with what she is doing."

Bob is pleased by the fact that his son Bob has now entered the insurance field. "We have a policy against nepotism," he explains, "so he started selling for Metropolitan Life, where he was recently promoted to agency manager. I have tried to stay very close to his activities since he started in the business, so the two of us frequently exchange ideas about the industry. It's interesting to see that while there have been many changes in the insurance field since I began my career, the reasons why people buy life insurance are still basically the same. The fundamental human emotions haven't changed. In fact, often I'll attend a meeting—sales, underwriting, or general agency, perhaps—and I'll see a speaker get up on the platform and really turn the audience on with what they think is a brand-new concept. I always listen closely—I'm interested in what they're saying—but sometimes I'll be smiling inwardly; because more often than not I'm hearing a message I might have heard twenty or thirty years ago. And there's nothing wrong with that at all. It's a matter of getting back to the basics. To paraphrase Vince Lombardi: You don't go too far from the blocking and tackling if you want to produce a winning team."

Bob advises his son and other young agents he talks to on the importance of becoming involved in professional organizations. "There are two good reasons for this," he stresses. "First, it's a great opportunity for personal growth. You can't be insulated to the point where you only get strength and educational information from within your own company. Even a company as large and productive as Pru isn't enough. There are many good minds around the world, and you want to come in contact with them so you can trade ideas and learn. This kind of exchange is crucial to your growth. Second, I believe in association work because I feel each of us has a responsibility to give something back to the industry. It's just as important to be a contributor as a receiver. It's a matter of paying your dues. I've always felt that I had something to pay back. And when I participate on a board, I want to get involved. I don't just make an appearance, I work at it. Anything less than full involvement is another wasted moment—and it's drudgery, besides. As far as I'm concerned, it's when I roll up my sleeves and really get to it that I have my fun."

Bob's own extensive civic activities demonstrate his belief that, as he says, "Each of us has a responsibility to try and make it a better world. I don't have any sympathy with people who plead, 'I can't make that much difference, so why bother?' Each of us can make a difference. We have to decide how much we're willing to put into it, and then go out and do it. This is part of our responsibility for being on this earth. And when you do get involved and active, you begin to make things happen, and you're going to enjoy it."

Looking back over his own career, Bob is quick to say that he believes luck can be a factor. "It's the old story about being in the right place at the right time. You know, it took me a long time to get a good mental fix on the fact that no matter what I did the day might still come when they preferred someone else over me. This is something you have to accept if you're shooting for the brass ring in a big corporation. A time can come in the development of a company when a style different than yours may be what's most needed at a given time. That can always happen, and if it does, that's the luck of the draw.

"But then," he adds, breaking out in a grin, "I have to say I still believe in the old philosophy that 'the harder I work, the luckier I get.' It's a time-worn phrase, but that's because it says it so well. I think that if you really take the total span of a lifetime, the luck factor will even itself out. Nobody consistently has that much good luck or bad luck. Over the long haul, a manager has to be judged by the results of his organization. And, given enough time, a good manager will always get good results, and a poor one will get poor results. There's no exception to it. All the luck gets washed out over time. I've seen poor managers take over a good organization and run it down the tubes. Likewise, a good manager can take over a weak organization, and given enough time and resources, he'll eventually get good results. The only thing that can affect him is his own attitude. If he lets his attitude suffer because of the problems he's trying to solve, he'll end up being a poor manager. But with good attitudes, good people always get good results."

One of the important factors in achieving good results in an organization, Bob believes, is careful implementation of new ideas. "It's good to have many programs and concepts," he states, "but you can't implement them all at once. The worst thing a professional manager can do is keep dropping new ideas on people without giving them a chance to learn them well enough to get results. Often the idea is not the hard part; the implementation is. Creativity is marvelous, as long as it produces a useful result. If it doesn't, who needs it? And good implementation takes time. You have to accept the fact that it may take a year or more just to get one good concept absorbed into the organization."

Although Bob advanced rapidly to the chairmanship of the largest insurance company in the world, he never felt intimidated by any new position. "In all truth, I've never felt like any job was too much to handle," he says, "and I've never really felt pressured or under stress. From what I've seen, the ability to feel comfortable with pressure is shared by the vast majority of senior managers. You have to be able to make a decision and not worry about it once it's been made. Sure, I may spend a lot of time thinking about it and turning it this way and that before I decide; but once a decision is made, it's made, and I'm not going to lie awake worrying about it. A senior manager must accept the responsibility of command, and realize that as long as he's mostly right, it's okay.

"This is especially important because a senior executive may not know the impact of his decisions for some time. Most of what's done in the higher echelons of management is not solving today's problems but solving tomorrow's. And certainly we dedicate ourselves to the growth of the company and the improvement of service. I know I have a dream for Prudential. I'd like what we do to have a really significant impact on society—enough so people will be able to say that the world is a somewhat better place because we've been here.

"Another thing a CEO has to live with is the knowledge that *the buck stops here.* There's no other place to go. I can get inputs from everybody under the sun, but in the final analysis, it's the CEO who makes the decision; he's responsible whether he actually makes it or not. If he has delegated it to others in the organization, he's still responsible. So it takes courage to delegate. No doubt about it, there's a lot of heat. I have seen CEOs from time to time who couldn't withstand these pressures. They didn't last very long."

One task many people would find burdensome is that of making frequent speeches. But Bob thoroughly enjoys this duty. However, more and more when he's called upon to talk to a group of Prudential agents or employees, he avoids giving a long, formal speech. Instead, he talks for only five to ten minutes and then opens the floor for questions. Long ago he realized that people were often hesitant to ask about the things they really wanted to know in front of a large group. For that reason, Bob instituted a policy of having questions written anonymously on index cards in advance of the speech and collected. He himself never sees them until he's in front of the audience. "You'd be surprised," he says, "at the questions people will ask with this system, things they'd be too inhibited to ask on a face-to-face basis—especially in front of a large group."

One question that comes up with increasing frequency is how Bob feels about growing government regulation of industry. "I'm not opposed to regulation *per se,*" he emphasizes. "I *am* opposed to regulation that is naive or politically inspired, regulation that interferes with the marketplace and causes the productivity of the nation to go down. Some regulation can be evaluated for the definite cost-benefit relationship. But you can't evaluate the destructive effect of regulation on the entre-preneurial attitude, and the elimination of some investment which is never made. When the government takes the incentive away from investment, the whole nation loses."

He shakes his head. "You can see it everywhere. We're losing in the area of technology. We're losing in the critical areas of innovation and creativeness. In the area of paperwork alone you can see the mess we've gotten into. If we did nothing else to improve the paperwork scene but require the person who designs a form to complete the form, we'd make great progress. They say they've improved the short form income tax return so a high school youngster can complete it. The facts simply do not support that statement. And it's so wasteful. There's no way to calculate how much all this seeps into the muscles and sinews of an organization, and what it does to people's willingness to go out and work and produce. Sure, there are areas in which the government does need to be in-volved, but it's gotten out of hand. It's becoming more and more difficult for us to compete with other nations; and that is a very serious concern for all of us."

It takes an unusual individual to deal with the myriad prob-lems, often national or international in scope, that confront the CEO of a major corporation today. Bob Beck is an unusual man. He loves a challenge and thrives on a sixteen-hour day. At fifty-four, he is rather young to be a CEO, so mandatory retirement is some time in the future. But his planning extends to his personal life, too. In his study at home is a file that holds slips of paper with all the things he would like to do when he does retire. "I want to write a book," he says. "I want to read *The Story of Civilization* by the Durants. I think I really might like to go to law school; that's something I've often thought about." What else is there? He laughs. "Every-thing. This file just keeps getting bigger all the time." There seems little doubt that Bob Beck's retirement will be just as spectacularly successful—and just as much fun—as his career has been.

2

Charles L. Brown

CHAIRMAN OF THE BOARD
AND CHIEF EXECUTIVE OFFICER,
AMERICAN TELEPHONE AND TELEGRAPH COMPANY

Charles Brown was first employed by AT&T as a construction worker during the summers of 1939 and 1941. He became a full-time equipment maintenance man for the company's Long Lines Department in Hartford, Connecticut, in May 1946. He held Long Lines assignments in New York, Birmingham, Atlanta, Philadelphia, Cincinnati, and Kansas City until June 1961, when he became an administrator at the company's Data Communications Center in Cooperstown, New York. In April 1962, he was made general manager of the Long Lines Central Area in Cincinnati, and in April 1963 he became general manager of the Southeastern Area located in Atlanta.

In July 1963, he was named vice president and general manager of the Illinois Bell Telephone Company in Chicago, and in March 1965 was elected vice president of operations. He was elected president of Illinois Bell in April 1969. In July 1974, he moved to New York City, where he was named executive vice president of AT&T. In April 1976, he was elected to the position of vice chairman and chief financial officer, and in April 1977 he became president of AT&T.

He became chairman of the board and chief executive officer of American Telephone and Telegraph Company on

February 1, 1981. With assets in excess of $125 billion, AT&T is the largest company in the world. For the twelve-month period ending December 31, 1981, the company had revenues exceeding $50 billion and a net income of $6.08 billion.

In addition to serving on AT&T's board of directors, Charlie is also a board member of E. I. Du Pont de Nemours & Company, Inc., and Chemical Bank and Chemical New York Corp. He is a director of the Associates of the Harvard University Graduate School of Business Administration. He is a trustee of Columbia Presbyterian Hospital, the Institute for Advanced Study at Princeton University, and the Colonial Williamsburg Foundation. He is a member of Delta Upsilon, Theta Tau, Omicron Delta Kappa, the Business Council, and the Business Roundtable.

He has served as a director for several Bell companies and also for GATX, Marcor, Inland Steel Company, Harris Bankcorp, and Hart Schaffner & Marx.

Charlie is also a past director of the Better Business Bureau; Community Fund of Chicago, Presbyterian Home in Chicago; Boy Scouts of America, Chicago Council; the Economic Club in Chicago; Lake Forest Hospital; and the Chicago Travelers Aid Society, which he also served as president. He is a past trustee of Lake Forest College and the University of Chicago; Chicago Educational Television Association; Chicago's Museum of Science and Industry; The Seeing Eye, Inc., in Morristown, N.J.; the Committee for Economic Development; and the Committee for Corporate Support of Private Universities.

He served as chairman for Illinois Citizens for Clean Water; Crusade of Mercy; Illinois Council on Economic Education Governing Board; and the Loyola University Board of Lay Trustees. He has also been a member of the Chicago Urban League Business Advisory Council; MERIT Employment Steering Committee; Northwestern University Associates Advisory Committee; Chicago's United Settlement Appeal Sponsoring Board; University of Chicago Citizens Board;

YMCA Advisory Board; Committee for Economic and Cultural Development of Chicago; Council of Financial Executives; and the Advisory Council of the Graduate School of Business, Columbia University.

Charlie graduated from the University of Virginia with a BS in electrical engineering in 1943. He attended the University of Pennsylvania Institute of Humanistic Studies for Executives in 1953.

Born in Richmond, Virginia, on August 23, 1921, Charlie lives with his wife, Ann Lee, in New Jersey. His son, Charles A. Brown, is a physician in Bakersfield, California.

CHARLES L. BROWN

Superior Fototech, Inc.

The name "Charlie Brown," popularized by the comic strip *Peanuts,* rings a bell with just about everyone. Yet in real life, far more bells ring every day on the lines of AT&T, a company headed by a *real* Charlie Brown. In fact, AT&T carries over 750 million messages a day via its 138 million telephones—over three and a half calls for every man, woman, and child in the United States. Perhaps no other company has so much impact on our daily lives.

While the name is the same, AT&T's Charlie Brown couldn't be more different from the insecure, inept round-headed cartoon character portrayed by Charles Schulz. In fact, his decisive, deft leadership is just what one would expect of a man who heads a company which is not just the largest purveyor of communications services anywhere, but the largest company of any kind in the world. The company presently employs more than a million people. The excellence of this unique company—one of the few non-government-operated telephone systems in the world—is a tribute to the company's history of effective management, as well as to the free enterprise system that makes it possible.

Charles L. Brown became the fourteenth CEO in AT&T's ninety-five-year history when he replaced John D. deButts in

1979. Since 1946, when his three-year term in the U.S. Navy ended, Charlie has spent his entire working career in the company. Even before that, during the summer of 1939, he worked as a thirteen-dollar-a-week ditch digger with an AT&T construction gang, putting up telephone poles. "It gave me some spending money"—he smiles—"and the pay wasn't as bad as it sounds. Because it was a traveling gang, we were furnished our room and board as we moved across the country."

Charlie was by no means the first in his family to work for AT&T. His mother had been employed there before her marriage, and his father logged thirty-seven years with the company. "He never tried to directly influence me to work for the telephone company," Charlie says, "but I knew how loyal he was to it. When I took the construction job, I thought it would be a chance to learn a little more about the company from another point of view. And then the job and the experience were both attractive; it was the first time I had ever traveled on my own." Charlie's experience led him to choose AT&T, although he considered a number of other companies. "Only when I had made the decision," he reminisces, "did my father let me know how much it meant to him. He was relieved and very pleased."

The possibility of working for the telephone company was in the back of Charlie's mind even in his college days. "I wanted to be in electrical engineering," he says, "and I knew there were many places within the telephone company where I could use that knowledge." In an age in which thousands of MBAs with aspirations to senior management graduate every year, could electrical engineering still provide a good start in career management? "I think so," Charlie replies. "An individual should be very good at what he does when he enters business, whatever his specialty might be. Then, if he can accompany that expertise with hard work and some good luck, he's going to move up in the organization. Yes, I think there are a lot a different routes to the top, and the one I took is a very satisfactory one.

"I would supplement this, however," he adds. "I happened

to have the good fortune to spend a full academic year at the University of Pennsylvania in 1953. I was in the Institute of Humanistic Studies for Executives, a program co-sponsored by the Bell System and the university, in which executives took a year off to concentrate on broad humanistic studies. I was very grateful for this opportunity; it widened my horizons immeasurably. The humanistic studies, combined with my technical background, gave me a new slant on the business, and it's been immensely helpful."

Certainly his education and experience have been important factors in making Charlie the right person to head AT&T. His many years of experience in various positions have given him a thorough working knowledge of the technical aspects of the business. At least as important has been the attitude he brings to his work. He believes enthusiasm is a necessary ingredient to doing any job well—and that includes running the largest company in the world. "Enthusiasm is the key to success in most endeavors," he stresses, "along with drive, competitiveness, persistence, and strength. The keen desire to accomplish your tasks is infectious. If a chairman is enthusiastic, it sets the tone for the whole organization."

The quality of leadership seems to come naturally to Charlie, although he tends to wave aside discussion of his accomplishments. A class officer in both high school and college, he lettered in and captained baseball and basketball teams. His athletic participation at the University of Virginia included freshman basketball and four years of baseball. At age sixty, still trim and athletic, he plays singles tennis twice a week and enjoys squash and golf now and then. "I like to compete," he says. "It gives me a great deal of satisfaction to play hard." If no competition is available, he enjoys just running his Airedale for exercise.

The determination and spirit Charlie brings to everything are illustrated when he tells of his physical examination for the Navy. The previous year, as a senior in college, he had become aware of a peculiar eye condition. His left eye saw short and his right eye saw long. "I couldn't hit a curve ball"—

he grins—"but I could read with one eye and look out for trucks with the other."

With the country at war, Charlie was determined not to let this condition disqualify him from service. "When it came to the eye exam," he recounts, "a very bored yeoman told me to put my hand over my left eye and read the chart. So I did. Then he told me to put my hand over my right eye and read the chart, and I read it and I passed. He wasn't paying much attention, or he would have seen that I didn't change eyes—I just changed hands." Charlie hastens to say that he isn't proud of that unusual instance of craftiness on his part. "But I was young," he says, "and I suppose I felt I knew more about whether I ought to go into the Navy than the Navy did."

The conservatively dressed executive seems far away from college and military days now, but reminders of the past decorate his office; among them is a twenty-foot pike. "That's what we used on the line gangs to raise and position telephone poles," he explains. The pike is a keepsake presented to Charlie by his associates at Illinois Bell on the occasion of his departure for AT&T's New York headquarters. Other souvenirs include a photograph of the University of Virginia, and an aerial view of the U.S.S. *Mississippi,* the battleship on which Charlie served in the Pacific theater.

The walls also hold mementos of business trips abroad: a small rug from Iran and an Egyptian painting. A golden samurai helmet, gift of the Nippon Electric Company Limited of Japan, is prominently displayed. Charlie's office is the one he moved into when he became president of AT&T. In 1979, when he assumed the chairmanship, he chose not to move down the hall to the office occupied by his predecessors, beginning with the company's first chairman, Theodore Vail. "I'm comfortable here," he says matter-of-factly. "Why get involved with all the headaches and expense of a move?" From these spacious offices on the twenty-sixth floor, overlooking the Brooklyn Bridge, come decisions that will institute change in the biggest company in the world and therefore in the lives of many Americans.

The sheer size of AT&T does not overwhelm Charlie and never has, whatever position he held. He is aware that people worry about being "a small cog in a machine," but he himself has never felt that way. "There's a popular image," he remarks, "that the individual in a large corporation is absorbed into some kind of soulless apparatus. But as far as I have been concerned, there have always been so many things I could do in each position, and so much to learn, that I've never felt constricted. I've always been stimulated by the learning experience of every position I've held. And if there was nothing more to learn about the immediate work I was involved in, I would look around me and find a great many things I knew nothing about."

The silver-haired executive has obviously had to learn a great deal about the telephone business during his thirty-four years with AT&T. In that time he has held twenty-three positions, sometimes moving rapidly from one to another. When asked whether he was always given enough time to thoroughly grasp a position before being moved on, he answers, "I can't say I've mastered every job I've been in. But I think it's characteristic of people who move up in this business that they are able to seize upon the essentials of a job quickly. If they weren't, they wouldn't be chosen for the positions. And it's reasonably common, not only here but elsewhere in business, that individuals who get to the top echelons have been in a good many places with many different kinds of jobs.

"Being exposed to so much of the business through my different positions has been very helpful," he continues. "It's true that AT&T has had CEOs whose careers were strictly at headquarters. Mr. Gifford, for example, one of the men who held this position the longest, had a background in finance and never had the benefit of diversified experience. Nevertheless, he did an excellent job. But in recent years we've tried to give promising people a broad background; we think it's exceptionally valuable. It's very difficult to administer properly unless you have a thorough grasp of jobs in the front line." While it is not uncommon today for corporations to seek top management outside the company, Charlie doesn't think this is likely to happen at AT&T. "It's always seemed to me," he asserts, "that a company has just plain failed in the development of its people if it's not able to find somebody inside to do the job."

After World War II, Charlie's career with AT&T began in the Long Lines Department, that part of the Bell System which connects the individual states and various Bell companies throughout the country. For example, a call from New York to Alabama goes through Long Lines facilities. Private long-distance lines are also part of Long Lines, as is overseas service. Charlie explains that long-distance service is one of the more profitable areas of the telephone business, and in fact helps support local service. In general, about seventy-five cents of a regular out-of-state phone call goes to support local service.

Charlie left Long Lines in 1961 to teach in Cooperstown, New York, at the company's Data Communications Training Center, where he became the school's first marketing dean. He smiles, recalling his time at the school. "It's ironic," he says. "As a college ball player, I always dreamed of someday ending up in Cooperstown, which, of course, is where the Baseball Hall of Fame is located. Well, one way or another I got there. In fact, it turned out to be a delightful town, and became my son's favorite of all the places we lived."

The fact that Charlie was sent for this training indicates that he was on a list of promotable people by that point in his career. Each company within the Bell System has such a list, based on the evaluations of immediate supervisors. Charlie explains that as positions open up, these people are given jobs that will test their abilities. Because the telephone business is highly measured, performance on many jobs can be quite accurately evaluated. An individual on the promotable list is assessed by a number of different people, so that politicking is not a significant factor in promotion.

Of all the positions Charlie held in Long Lines, he most enjoyed his job as district plant superintendent in Birmingham,

Alabama, from 1952 through 1954. "I was working in a three-state area," he says, "Alabama, Mississippi, and Louisiana, and I really liked that part of the country. And then I was just thirty-one years old, and it was my first opportunity to supervise a large number of people—about three hundred. I was also responsible for the maintenance of millions of dollars of long-distance equipment, so I really had my work cut out for me."

Although Charlie enjoyed this position most, he is quick to add that he enjoyed every job he has held within AT&T and has never had a chance to get bored. And although frequent transfers are not easy on a family, he believes the variety of his positions has given him a valuable perspective for his job as CEO. "Your view of the company broadens as you move into different facets of the business."

Charlie describes himself as competitive and ambitious all his life. "But I have never given much thought to where I would end up in the company," he says. "Of course, I always knew that the Bell System believes in developing its own people for higher positions. But I've been happy with the jobs I had, and it's been my objective to enjoy my present job and do well at it. It is absolutely not necessary to politick or step on anyone's neck to get ahead. Your results speak for themselves. You compete best by doing well at your job and proving your competence."

In July 1963, Charlie moved out of Long Lines to become vice president and general manager of Illinois Bell. By March 1965, he had become vice president of operations, and in April 1969 he was named president. He remained in Chicago in that position for five years. In July 1974, he was named executive vice president and chief financial officer, and he has worked out of AT&T's headquarters in New York ever since. In April 1976, he became vice chairman of the board; one year later he became president. In 1979, he assumed the position of chairman of the board.

To be CEO for the largest corporation in the world is an enormous responsibility, and it seems at first glance surprising that such a position could be filled by someone with a background in electrical engineering. "I think this is characteristic of the strength and depth that exists in this organization," Charlie says. "There's a great difference between administering a large organization which is a going concern and administering a small one where you do everything yourself. In this sort of business, a great deal is delegated. As chief financial officer, for instance, I had both treasury people and accounting people who reported to me; and they were very well equipped to carry on their end of the business. There's another factor, too, and that's the education I gained from moving around in various positions. You learn principles of administration you can apply to almost any job. You also learn what's important and what isn't."

Holding so many positions, Charlie was required to relocate a number of times during his career. While he believes that moving a few times can be a positive experience for a family, because of the exposure to different life-styles, he admits that there can come a point when it is detrimental. "By the fourth or fifth move, you lose a sense of roots," he says. "Instead of benefiting the family, the move can be disruptive. My wife, of course, has taken the worst of the beating. She became very good at absorbing the difficulties of moving into a new city; still, I'm sure it was a strain on her and the boy. For myself, I've always had the familiar surroundings of the business. The job, the location, and the people may be different, but the environment is generally the same. So I've always felt comfortable, and things would automatically fall into place for me."

The year 1963 was a particular strain for the Browns. In February, Charlie had been named general manager of the Long Lines Department's Southeastern Area and transferred to Atlanta. "I had lived there in 1954," he explains, "and I liked Atlanta very much. We purchased a home and moved our furniture in"—he sighs—"and ten days later I was offered a job as vice president and general manager of Illinois Bell, which meant we had to move to Chicago. Needless to say, that move was undertaken with mixed emotions."

Today a Bell employee who is transferred has the option of selling his house to the company at the market price. But in 1963 there was no such policy. As a result, during 1963 the Browns made five house transactions. "I sold a house in Cincinnati," Charlie explains, "bought and sold one in Atlanta, and then bought one near Chicago. Meanwhile, I managed to sell a house in Kansas City that we hadn't been able to sell when we left there. People told me I really ought to take out a real estate license!"

Through all this, Charlie's wife, Ann Lee, maintained her equilibrium. "She's been a major factor in my success," he affirms. "If a person has to worry about a tense situation at home, I imagine it would be very difficult to carry out a decent day's work. And in our business, the wife is very much a part of things. No matter where telephone people go—luncheons, cocktail parties—somebody will bring up the telephone business. The telephone is a part of everyone's life, and people often feel very deeply about it if something goes wrong. If they have a complaint about a bill or a service call, they are likely to tell not just their local service representative, but also anyone associated with the company.

"It's a peculiar fact about the telephone," he muses, "that people have very personal feelings about it. It's not like other products, probably because it's so important in linking people to the outside world. People who wouldn't complain about a repair bill on a washing machine will tell the world how they feel if their telephone service is not what they think it ought to be. I think in a way this sort of public reaction tends to draw telephone families closer together."

Charlie counts on spending time with his family on weekends. During the week, he typically works a fourteen-hour day. Up at six, he rides about eighty minutes from his home in New Jersey to his Manhattan office. Since the company supplies a driver, he can spend this time catching up on necessary reading. Because it is uninterrupted time, he finds it quite productive. Normally it is 8:00 P.M. before Charlie arrives back home. Once there he relaxes, rarely working evenings or weekends.

Charlie manages his enormous work load by delegating authority wherever he can. "And I try never to waste time on details," he says. "I'm not a detail person, and I have to depend on others to keep me from making blunders which are occasioned by not knowing in detail the facts of a given situation. The people who work with me understand this, and they know I depend on them to speak up without equivocation when they think I'm heading in the wrong direction. This has been a very satisfying way for me to operate, and they also seem to enjoy having an opportunity to directly influence policy."

Delegating authority has its inherent dangers, and Charlie is well aware of that. "This style of management has to be undertaken with extreme caution," he says. "In a company of this size, decisions may have great impact. They have to be the right decisions."

A senior executive close to Charlie says he is "as good a listener as anyone I know. Charlie's a man of few words, and he wastes no time in whatever he does. He has the knack of getting to the heart of any situation. He always asks the right questions."

Charlie himself claims this ability is typical of CEOs. "Those who head big operations," he says, "have to be able to filter out what's unimportant and concentrate on the real purpose. I'm sure most CEOs have developed the ability to do this before they ever take the position. You have to know how to ask the right questions to cut through the many unimportant things that take time and distract you from the issue at hand."

Charlie avoids the large, sometimes unproductive meetings which are a way of life in many corporations. "Some executives include everybody they can muster up." He shakes his head. "I want only those people who are necessary in order to arrive at a conclusion. Brisk, small meetings have a much better possibility of resulting in something than large ones.

"But I do want to emphasize," he adds, "that in a complicated business such as ours, many factors have to be taken into account. For instance, we may not be able to make a marketing decision without knowing the mechanical ability of the network or the plant to carry it out. We may need to know whether and how the regulatory authorities will enter the picture. We'll need to include the financial man. In any decision, there are a certain number of interlocking issues that can't be dispensed with. But I try not to let non-essential factors interfere with the decision-making process."

The affection Charlie's co-workers feel for him is accompanied by respect. "If you come to one of his meetings without being fully prepared," one executive says, "you're in for a rude awakening. He certainly won't call you down on it, but you'll know damn well how he feels. And you'll be so embarrassed that you'll never put yourself in that position again." Charlie does not deny how he feels about inadequate preparation. "I think one of the most debilitating things that can happen at a business meeting is to have a number of people in attendance who are not prepared, to whom the subject is vague. Not only are they wasting their time, they waste everyone's else's. And I don't like it."

Charlie's administrative style includes what has been referred to as "popping up in the damnedest places at the damnedest times." One executive recalls him showing up at a luncheon where a plant employee was getting a fifteen-year pin. Charlie, who comes across as quiet, almost shy, is perfectly capable of going down a manhole to talk to the person working there and ask if he's having any problems. From time to time he likes to stop by the switchboard and talk with the chief operator, or visit the computer room and ask questions. Even today, he will occasionally call a service representative to find out the facts on a problematical customer account. "This organization has so many facets," he says, "that you can only get a feel for it by going where the action is. I think talking to people on the line is the best way to get a feel for the total operation."

What Charlie refers to as "just sitting still and looking at the numbers" is, of course, an important part of his job. But he also emphasizes the area of human resources. "The overall administration of personnel is my ongoing responsibility," he says. In addition, he is heavily involved with public relations, finance, operations, manufacturing, and research. His responsibility to make decisions involving all these areas entails a great deal of reading. "I have to be on top of such things as what service and earnings results are," he explains, "what Bell Labs is coming up with, how it might mesh into our business, and what the competition is doing. There's that absorption of environment I've talked about before. And I spend a good deal of time on long-term planning, looking ahead to the next dozen years or so. We are vitally concerned about the future, so this is one of my primary interests. I also spend a fair amount of time addressing groups and attending conferences." One remaining area is unusually important to AT&T and therefore of prime concern to its CEO—legislation and government regulation. To keep on top of the changes in these areas, Charlie must spend a great deal of time in Washington.

In order to understand the time and energy devoted to government regulation, it is necessary to be familiar with the history of telephone service in America. Since early days, AT&T has been a regulated industry. The Communications Act of 1934 granted AT&T a regulated monopoly. In 1956, threatened with divestiture of various Bell units, AT&T signed a consent decree that allowed the company to keep Western Electric (which makes most of the telephone equipment) but required Bell to provide only regulated common carrier communications services.

Since the mid-1960s, AT&T has had increasing competition. In 1968, in the landmark Carterfone case, the FCC allowed the hookup of customer-owned equipment to the Bell System. AT&T and other telephone companies tried to get Congress to redefine their position in 1976 by supporting the Consumer Communications Reform Bill (dubbed the "Bell Bill" by critics), but the effort was stillborn. Two years later, Representative Lionel Van Deerlin (Democrat of California) sponsored the Communications Act of 1978, a complete rewrite of the Communications Act of 1934. Advocates argued that Bell was still being regulated by an act forty years old, in a time which has seen sweeping growth and change. This act would have forced AT&T to create arm's-length subsidiaries while allowing it more freedom to compete. In 1979, a revised version of the bill was introduced, which did not require divestiture.

On another front, the computer industry argued that the 1956 consent decree limits AT&T on data communications, making the company's increasing role in data processing illegal. The computer companies fear that Bell's communications processing business will be subsidized with profits from its telephone business, thus lending Bell an unfair advantage.

The legal and technical complexities of these problems make it necessary for Charlie to devote a major portion of his time to them. This period of change may be the most important in AT&T's long existence. Charlie states: "I would like to have it said that during my term I had a hand in getting the ground rules for telecommunications clarified, so the organization knows it can operate in a mixed competitive regulated environment. I would like to have it said that the company was restructured in a way that permitted it to readily adapt to customer needs in this period of competitive change. We're faced with the need for ground rules," he explains, "so we can understand where we stand and what we're facing. But instead of clear regulations, we have the continued uncertainty of an indecisive Washington. We face competition in every aspect of the business, but we're prohibited from competing on an equal level. Is it real competition when one company is regulated, as we are, and another is not? Is it real competition when one company has freedom of entrance into any aspect of our business, and we do not have freedom of exit from unprofitable business?"

Freedom of entry and exit is a problem peculiar to the telephone industry. AT&T itself is enjoined by law to provide certain services; some are minimally profitable. A competitor, on the other hand, can enter a highly profitable area of the business, such as long-distance service between major markets like New York and Chicago. "They skim the cream," Charlie says, "and they *don't* have to serve Broken Bow, Oklahoma. We do! I don't see any competitors for that job. Now, if there's going to be freedom of entry to the most profitable market-places, then freedom of exit should also apply to us.

"Let me emphasize that we are not against competition. Nor am I suggesting that we withdraw service from the low-density markets. This is a delicate situation which needs to be handled carefully. I *am* saying that it is obvious that some companies are treated differently from others."

AT&T has a more vulnerable position in regard to govern-ment regulation than most companies. Charlie stresses that he is not against necessary regulation. He does believe that in many areas there is overregulation, and he thinks the deregu-latory movement he sees building now will have a positive effect on the country. "In principle, regulators try to do good for the general public," he acknowledges. "But there is an insidious tendency to regulate more things than need regula-tion. By the time various agencies regulate equal opportunity, safety, health, and so on, you have to wonder whether business is left with enough control to do its job. The unfortunate part is that the regulators have virtually no accountability for the cost increases involved."

AT&T is very interested in the passage of a new Communica-tions Act. Charlie notes that this enormous company is operat-ing under regulations imposed by the 1934 Act, which has been modified to some extent over the years but is basically unchanged. "The worst part about it," he states, "is that policy is being made all along, and in an ad hoc sort of way. The FCC makes up its ideas as it goes along; the commission changes, the staff changes, and new rules are promulgated. The courts affect us, too, with their decisions. But the public, by virtue of its elected representatives, has not had a chance to get involved in the issue since 1934. And that's what we're trying to get at now—to have Congress speak definitively on the matter."

Charlie's approach to these problems is naturally compared

to that of John D. deButts, his predecessor. DeButts, one of the best-known and most outspoken business leaders in America during his six-year tenure as CEO, is a big, ebullient, somewhat overpowering man. His competitiveness was sometimes translated into a near-pugilistic stance which made enemies in Washington. In contrast, Charlie is a private, reserved, soft-spoken person. Associates have characterized him as more of a compromiser than deButts, willing to give and take. But, they add, "Charlie, too, is a fierce competitor. His willingness to compromise should never be interpreted as a lack of strength."

Charlie points out that consecutive CEOs are not necessarily stamped out of an identical mold. Because he and deButts worked in the same operating telephone company, some people believe they must think the same. But AT&T's needs have changed drastically in the recent past. "Unlike many businesses," Charlie says, "we have had to respond rapidly to change. Where we were formerly a regulated monopoly, we now have competition in almost every aspect of the business. It's an entirely different ball game than it was just a few years ago. The new managers have different problems to solve, and it is unlikely that we will think the same way or act the same way as our predecessors."

While he and deButts are different, Charlie denies that they are as different as people sometimes think. "From my long association with John," he says, "I know he is not as stubborn, arrogant, and uncompromising as his detractors would lead people to think. By the same token, anyone who believes I'm a patsy is badly mistaken. John and I are not as different as all that. I *do* face a different environment than he did, and I have to deal with it differently. I think the job of helping the organization to be agile in an era of rapid change is a very important part of my work. My successors will either bless or curse me for this company's agility in response to change over the next few years."

As a regulated monopoly, AT&T must be alert to public opinion and need. "If we're not responsive to what the public wants," Charlie says, "then we're not doing our job. We're very concerned about how we're regarded. We constantly ask the public what they think about us in many, many ways. We want to know how they feel about the prices, whether they think we're too big. Generally, we find a high acceptance of the service we're providing."

Typically, the American public dislikes large institutions of any kind—unions, business, or government. "The general feeling of the answers," Charlie says, "is, 'Yes, you're very big, and we wish you didn't have to be, but we see the need.' People do realize that telephone service could not be rendered by a large number of small shopkeepers. So we find no public sentiment for breaking up this company. The public recognizes that we're large, and they wish we could be smaller; but they accept the necessity."

There are those who think AT&T's $6 billion in annual profits is excessive if not outrageous. Charlie points out that the rate of return on the capital invested in the business, including the debt and the equity, is in fact 9.5 percent. "It's as if you invested a hundred dollars in a candy store," he says, "and you got nine dollars and fifty cents return at the end of the year. That's what it boils down to. You just put some more zeros on the end, that's all. I think anyone who examines it can see that it isn't unreasonable."

But profit, Charlie stresses, is not AT&T's primary objective. "This is a different kind of business," he reflects. "The people in this company—not only me, but others—understand that we operate a business that's essential to the public interest. These jobs carry with them a responsibility which is really like a public trust. We cannot let the public telephone system go bad in this country, and we will not. For many of us, it's a deeply felt personal responsibility. We have to keep this company sensitive to America's needs. Our job is to provide good service. If we don't do that, it doesn't make any difference what else we do."

3

Richard J. Ferris

PRESIDENT AND CHIEF EXECUTIVE OFFICER, UAL, INC.

After earning his bachelor's degree at Cornell University in 1962, Richard Ferris joined Western International Hotels in Seattle as a staff planner. In 1966, he was named general manager of the Continental Plaza Hotel in Chicago. After serving in various capacities for Western International Hotels, Dick headed United's new Food Services Division after Western was merged with UAL, Inc., in 1970. In January 1974, he was named the airline's chief marketing officer, and later the same year was elected president.

He was elected chief executive officer of UAL, Inc., in April 1979. He became president of this holding company in April 1978, and has been chairman of the board of the company's largest subsidiary, United Airlines, since December 1978. He had been elected president of the nation's biggest airline in December 1974 and named its chief executive officer in April 1976.

Dick is a member of the Board of Directors of UAL, Inc., and its subsidiary companies United Airlines, Western International, and GAB Business Services. He is also a director of the Procter and Gamble Company.

A director and member of the Air Transport Association, he serves on the boards of the Transportation Association of America, Evanston Hospital, National Merit Scholarship Corporation, Project Orbis, Inc., and on the national board of United Way of America.

He is also a member of the Business Roundtable, the Business Advisory Committee, Transportation Center, Northwestern University, and the Cornell University Council. Business organizations he is affiliated with include the Chicago Association of Commerce and Industry; the Economic Club of Chicago; Executives' Club (Chicago); The Wings Club, Inc. (New York); and the Conference Board.

Dick served for three years in the U.S. Army prior to entering Cornell University. He was born on August 31, 1936, in Sacramento, California. He and his wife, Kelsey, live in suburban Chicago with their three sons—Andrew, Brian, and Mark.

When Dick Ferris graduated from Hotel School at Cornell University, he decided he was too old to take more time out for his master's degree just then. "I was twenty-five," he says, gesturing expansively. "It was time to get going, time to get to work!"

With his eye on one day becoming the general manager of a hotel, Dick took a job running the Olympic Grill at Seattle's Olympic Hotel, a Western International hotel. Twelve years later, he had overshot his goal by a mile to become president of the biggest airline in the country, United. At age forty-two, he topped himself when he was elected chief executive officer of UAL, Inc., the $4 billion parent company of both United and Western International. Dick Ferris had quickly made up for what he considered a late start.

While it was not in his original plan, Dick's move from the hotel industry to airlines was a smooth one. In the course of his meteoric career, he had become used to major leaps. Whether a promotion took him to South Africa or to a totally new area of responsibility, he accepted it in stride. "I just kept my eye on my work," the handsome young executive says with a slight shrug.

His entry into the hotel industry was paved by a series of

events that began in his youth, when he worked during the summer at Lake Tahoe. "For a young guy, working at a resort on the lake was *the* thing to do," he says. Dick started out as a houseman, cleaning rooms; later he waited on tables. After he graduated from high school, Dick enlisted in the Army and ended up in Tokyo, in Troop Information and Education. Because he was a qualified swimming instructor, he was transferred into Special Services. Later he was put to work at Tokyo's Rocker Four Club, one of the Army's largest NCO clubs. This was his first real exposure to the hospitality business.

By the age of twenty, Dick was the manager of the Rocker Four Club. There he met Frank Ready, president of the Japanese chapter of the Cornell Society of Hotelmen, a worldwide organization. (Ready, a graduate of the Cornell Hotel School, came from a family with a tradition of hotel work; his father, in fact, had built New York's Waldorf-Astoria.) At Ready's invitation, Dick went to a meeting of the society. The meeting, conducted by Ichira Inamuru, son of the founder of the Imperial Hotel, and attended by Japan's leading hoteliers, fascinated Dick. "It was as though somebody had turned a light bulb on in my head!" he says happily. "They got me so excited about the hotel business that I was sure it was my big chance in life. I was twenty-one, and it was time to decide on my career. I knew this was it."

In high school, Dick had been a mediocre student, without motivation or direction. Now he determined to try to get into the world's finest school of hotel management. He took his college boards while he was still in Japan and did well enough to achieve his goal—he was accepted at Cornell.

His years there were a happy blur of work and study. The first year he worked at the Statler Inn as sommelier, beginning a long love affair with fine wines. Later he advanced to the position of beverage manager. His senior year, he was named managing director of HEC, the equivalent of the class presidency. HEC (Hotel Ezra Cornell, named after the founder of the university) is an annual weekend affair where the students run a hotel, seminars, and banquets, and invite alumni

RICHARD J. FERRIS

to attend. Dick had received numerous job offers at this point, as do almost all Cornell students, and he had decided to go with Western International Hotels. A small company, Western had ambitious plans and an entrepreneurial philosophy of management that Dick liked. "And the chemistry was good between their people and myself," he adds. Furthermore, Western was headquartered in Seattle, and Dick wanted to return to the west.

At the HEC banquet, Dick talked to Dan London, who managed Western's St. Francis Hotel. Dick's admiration for this man, called "Mr. San Francisco," led him to say, "What I *really* want to do when I begin with Western is work with you."

"No you don't," London told him. "You want to work at the Olympic in Seattle, where everybody at headquarters can see you. Because if you do it right, more people will know it than just me. Of course, if you do it wrong, it'll be all over. But," he added, "knowing you, I'm sure you'll do all right. Go to Seattle." Dick took his advice, and began with Western an manager of the Olympic Grill for the famous Seattle hotel.

In Seattle, Dick met his wife, Kelsey, who was secretary for the Olympic's resident manager. The two years there were hectic ones, as Dick decided to pursue his master's degree. The couple got up at six, and Kelsey drove Dick to the Olympic in their Volkswagen. Then she went on to her new job at the Benjamin Franklin Hotel, since in those days Western's policy did not allow a married couple to work together. Dick worked from seven to one in the restaurant and as staff planner for the hotel. At one, Kelsey picked him up and drove him to the university, eating her lunch in the car. There he would attend classes and study until five, when she picked him up again to take him back to his work at the hotel. At nine-thirty, she would pick him up a third time, and he would go home to study until midnight.

Dick was nearly through his master's studies when Western offered him the first of many transfers. The Savoy Plaza in New York was slated for demolition; in the meantime, Western managed it for some British interests. They wanted Dick to go there as assistant to the general manager.

"What a terrific experience!" Dick says. "There we were, newly married, living in a suite at the grand old Savoy Plaza. We loved it. I had all sorts of friends from Cornell who lived in New York, and Kelsey got a job just up the street, so everything was going smoothly."

Young, bright, and enthusiastic, Dick did so well at his work that he caught the attention of Ed Carlson, Western's chairman, and Gordon Bass, its president. Much later Carlson told Dick what happened then. "They thought I looked too good to be true," Dick relates. "Eddie said, 'Let's test him. Let's see if he's got the stuff.' So," Dick recalls, "with a great deal of malice aforethought, they yanked me out of the Savoy and sent me to Anchorage, Alaska!"

"Now, can you imagine what it's like to be transferred from Manhattan to Anchorage?" he asks with a wide grin. "I can still hear my friends calling me.

" 'Hi, Dick, what's new? '

" 'Oh, not much,' I'd say, knowing darn well that they had already heard the news.

" 'Really? I heard you were being transferred.'

" 'Oh, yeah, well, that's true.'

" 'Where to, Dick?' And you *knew* they knew.

" 'Anchorage, Alaska,' I'd have to say.

" '*Anchorage, Alaska!*' To them that was the end of the world."

So Kelsey and Dick went to Alaska, where he worked as food and beverage manager at the luxurious 800-room Anchorage-Westward Hotel. They found Alaska, far from being "the end of the world," a wonderful state to live in and wouldn't trade the experience for anything.

Fifteen months later, in 1966, Dick was transferred to Chicago, where he was named executive assistant manager of the Continental Plaza, one of the largest and most profitable Western hotels, and one of the few the company then owned outright. For a man with only three years of full-time work experience, Dick was being given a great deal of responsibility.

Four months later, at age twenty-eight, he was given even more—he became general manager of the Continental Plaza. "For a college student of hotel management," he says, "this is a lifetime dream—to manage a major hotel. And when you're with an organization like Western, it's a fantastic opportunity. Their philosophy is to allow the hotel manager to run his own business, exactly as an entrepreneur would. He works with people, both the employees and the clientele. He deals with the financial end of the business, from determining his own cash flow to handling his own capital improvement program. It's *his* business, his own $6, $12, $15 million business. Today, of course, some of them are $50 million businesses—like the Plaza in New York.

"So at a very early age," he recalls enthusiastically, "I was able to move out of the textbook world of business and into a position where I was responsible for financial, legal, production, and personnel matters. It was my ball game—a wonderful experience."

Undoubtedly this kind of broad experience is an excellent preparation for the job of CEO. Dick is aware that many corporations are structured so that their people do not get such broad exposure. "It's nobody's fault," he says. "It's a result of the size and specialization of the corporation. But when young people move up in a functional-oriented direction, their focus is very narrow. They don't seem to see the other sides of the business that bring the whole picture together. So I consider myself very fortunate to have had the experience I did with Western."

After "two great years" in Chicago, Dick was chosen to head operations in Johannesburg, South Africa, where Western was building the 600-room Carlton Hotel. Although they now had two young sons, Dick and Kelsey were eager to make the move. The hotel in Johannesburg and one in Bangkok were Western's first international ventures. "We thought it would be a wonderful experience to live in another country," Dick explains. "And I was enjoying what I was doing. My attitude was 'If that's what they want me to do, I'll do it.'

"Now, here," he continues, in a lowered voice, "is a good place to mention a very important element in my life—Eddie Carlson. He was the chairman of Western, and he was the man who had recognized me after my first two years with the company and, along with some others, caused my career to advance very rapidly. I didn't really know it at the time, but each new assignment was a test. And when I had performed, he continued to accelerate the pace and give me additional responsibility.

"Eddie had faith in me, and I've always been grateful for that. He had an expression, 'I can open the door for you, but you've got to walk through it.' Well, I was lucky to have a guy who was willing to open the door. I can't say enough for that. I was very fortunate to work in a climate where I was able to develop, allowed to make mistakes, and encouraged to succeed."

Dick began his assignment in Johannesburg with zest. The Carlton would be a gorgeous hotel, a world-class hotel. But after a while it became obvious that the project wasn't moving as rapidly as had been projected. "We had this huge hole in the ground," he says, wincing, "and it just sat there. I could picture myself spending five years down here before this hotel opened."

At the end of his first year in Johannesburg, Dick found out that Eddie and the vice chairman, Lynn Himmelman, were scheduled to be in Paris, where they had been working on a hotel project. Dick sent them a cable: "Kelsey and I will be on vacation in Greek Islands. Understand you will be in Paris in September. Will see you there. Want to talk with you. Dick."

In September, Dick showed up at the Bristol Hotel in Paris. "Eddie and Lynn took me aside for a private meeting," he recalls, "and I told them that I wanted to leave South Africa because I didn't feel I was being productive for the corporation—or for myself. I told them, 'A year from now it will probably be appropriate, and I could return at that time. But right now you ought to use me differently.'

"To show you what kind of person Eddie is," Dick says affectionately, "he changed his whole travel schedule to spend twenty-four hours in South Africa looking into the situation. Then he met with our partners, the Anglo-American Corporation, and told them it would be most appropriate to have me taken out at that time and to reassign me later. And at the time, I thought I would return. Then Eddie went on to Bangkok."

Kelsey and Dick returned to Seattle, where for the next year Dick worked as a project officer in the construction of new hotels. The position required him to coordinate all facets of construction, including dealing with the architects and general contractors. In some instances, he took a hotel through the whole construction process, beginning with input into the decision as to which market would support a new hotel, followed by the actual construction, and then finally by working with the operational crew which would take over the business of managing the hotel. The projects he worked on included the Houston Oaks, the Winnipeg Inn in Calgary, and studies on the Continental Plaza in Chicago that eventually led to a major addition to the hotel. Just before the new tower at the Bayshore Inn in Vancouver, British Columbia, was scheduled to open, the manager resigned, and Dick was called to act as its manager. "There had been a story going around the company," he comments, "that they never let me open one. Well, I finally got to!"

While Dick was project officer, his family lived in a rented home with rented furniture in Seattle, using silver and china borrowed from the hotel (many of their possessions were still in Johannesburg). Then in 1970, Western formed a partnership with Don and Joyce Hall, the owners of Hallmark, to build Crown Center, Kansas City's magnificent hotel. Appointed general manager, Dick moved with his family to Kansas City in April 1971.

"I told Kelsey we were going to be there for the next four years," Dick explains, "so why not build our own home? We had three children now, but it was to be our first home, and naturally she was very excited. So we built it and worked with a decorator, and the place was just perfect. One day in August, she called me up—the decorator had just hung the last picture. She was so thrilled.

"Well, that day I got a call from Eddie Carlson. They wanted me in Chicago. We had moved ten times in ten years, and that was the first time a move had got to her. I called her and said, 'Guess what?' and she burst into tears. Finally she said, 'Well, where are we going now?' We both really love Chicago, so when I told her she stopped crying.

"It's kind of funny looking back on it now. When we got married, and then made that first move from Seattle to New York, she was in a state of shock. It had never occurred to her that her husband would have to move. But she's been a real trouper. She's been absolutely supportive throughout my entire career."

Dick pauses briefly. "You don't have to be married to be successful, but if you are married, you have to have a supportive wife. If you're not happy at home, you don't perform as well at work. And if you're unhappy at work, you're not as good at home. Fortunately, Kelsey is a strong woman, and she keeps me in line. Now, I don't say you *have* to have a wonderful spouse to be successful. But if you don't, it's like being in a horse race and carrying a forty-pound handicap."

When the Ferris family moved to Chicago in 1971, it meant that Dick would be working at the world headquarters of UAL, Inc., which had bought Western International Hotels the previous September. Dick still vividly remembers the day he was told that Western had been acquired. "It was a very emotional day," he says, "and I'll never forget it. Eddie had called in every manager from all over the world, and that had never happened before. So we knew something very important was up. Then they told us there had been a friendly takeover by United.

"Well, there was a hush and then everybody was talking at once. 'United! An airline!' 'My God, we're being taken over by an airline!' The general reaction was a real fear that we might lose the standard of quality Western had always stood for. It was a sinking feeling. Everyone there felt the same, because we had all been developed from within; that was the way it was done at Western. So we had a lot of spirit and belief in what the company stood for. Western's hotels were very prestigious. We didn't want anything to change."

In September, the managers were reassured when Eddie Carlson and Lynn Himmelman were put on the boards of UAL, Inc., and United. Because of the conversion, they were probably the two largest individual shareholders of UAL stock. Three months later George Keck, CEO of UAL, Inc., resigned, and Eddie Carlson took over.

"That was when we really breathed a sigh of relief," Dick says with a smile. "Now there was someone we knew at the helm!"

Dick's first job with the airline was to head the Food Services Division. When the total number of meals served by United is calculated, the job entailed managing one of the largest food services in the world. Once again, Dick was given the freedom to succeed. His job was essentially to carve out this integral part of the airline and operate it as a separate division— at the very beginning of the divisional concept at United. "It goes back to Western's practice of letting a manager run his own hotel," Dick explains. "That's exactly the kind of thing we're attempting at United. Each division operates as a separate cost center, or perhaps profit center would be a more accurate description. We want to create an atmosphere that generates the entrepreneurial spirit in the people within the company.

"When I first took over Food Services," he continues, "I told our managers, in essence, 'Look, fellows, if you can't run this division efficiently, then we may as well close it down and buy food services somewhere else.' Then we developed a system to sell our product to the rest of the company. United buys 25 percent of what we use from other companies, and this establishes the going rate; Food Services is not permitted to charge any more or less than the other companies for the same meal. Now, those other companies have to lay their costs against their investment, and they're in business to make a profit. So in a sense, matching our product and our prices with theirs has made our Food Service very entrepreneurial."

The divisional concept encourages management to be creative. One of the first changes Dick made as head of Food Services was to incorporate some imagination. "We brought Trader Vic in," he says, beaming and gesturing. "We broke away from the traditional airline meal. We served tortellini and pastas. We stopped doing things just because 'that's the way it was always done.' We put some creativity into the menu-planning process. And we stressed good high-quality food that was well prepared and attractively presented.

"Now, to say that it's a gourmet experience to eat on United would be ridiculous. We weren't after that. We wanted to keep it simple. If you become too elaborate, well, face it, it won't work. When you cook your steak on the barbecue at home, you get upset if you overcook it or undercook it by one minute. Well, can you imagine cooking that steak and serving it four hours later and having it come out perfect? You know, the airlines do an absolutely remarkable job with food when you consider all the logistical problems involved."

Following his success with United's Food Services Division, Dick was promoted in January of 1974 to chief marketing officer. By December of the same year, he was president of United Airlines. In only twelve years, he had advanced from serving wine at the Olympic Grill in Seattle to being president of the largest airline in the country. His swift-moving career is certainly one of the most remarkable in the history of American business.

Dick does not find his transition from the hotel business to the airline business as remarkable as many outsiders do. Matter-of-factly, he points out the similarities. "First, both are service businesses, not manufacturers. Second, both have the exact same problem—a very perishable product. A bed not sold tonight or an airplane seat not sold today is gone forever. We cannot inventory it. Third, the channels of distribution are predominately the same, and so is the marketing.

Both industries rely on travel agents and the media. Then, of course, there are the other similarities which exist in every business. Wherever you go, economics is economics, finance is finance, accounting is accounting, and people are people." He adds parenthetically, "The *attitude* of our people, by the way, is one of the most important things we have to sell. And Eddie made that theme come alive at this airline—*the friendly skies.*

"But hotels and airlines both provide services," he continues. "Look at it this way. In the case of a hotel, we have a piece of property—a vertical building which provides lodging for our customers. Now, with an airplane, we have a silver tube—a highly technical, beautiful silver tube—that takes you from A to B through the air.

"Of course, there are significant differences, too. An airplane is a more complicated mechanism, demanding certain skills of the people who fly it. And it operates within the air traffic control system, and within the regulations of the federal government. Coming from a non-regulated industry, that was probably the biggest difference I found." Considering that the CEO of a highly regulated industry may spend 25 or even 50 percent of his time dealing with regulations, that difference is a large one. Dick shrugs and smiles. "It was just a matter of doing my homework, that's all."

Dick's characteristic determination to learn as much as possible about his work is well illustrated when he tells about the events that led him to earn his pilot's license. "I don't like to not understand something," he says, "and I think you ought to have a basic working knowledge of what you are trying to lead or direct. Now, I did have firsthand knowledge of what flight attendants do, because one summer while I was at Cornell I had worked as a steward for Pan American World Airways. But I didn't know anything about planes. So I decided that the best way to understand how a plane worked, and at the same time learn the air traffic control system, was to learn how to fly.

"Well, that was what I decided when I became president,

but I was working on a very busy schedule. Then, during a flight to Hawaii, I stopped up in the cockpit to say hello—which I always do—and introduced myself to the captain—Jack Starr. What a terrific name for a pilot!" Dick says, grinning. "Anyway, Jack, who was one of our most senior captains, asked me if I had ever wanted to learn to fly. I told him, 'Sure, I'd love to.' Then he asked if I would mind if he stopped by to discuss that with me, and I told him that would be fine.

"About two weeks later, my secretary came in and told me there was a Captain Starr to see me. Well, I told her to bring him in. He said he wondered if I was ready to go flying yet. He could have a plane ready any time at the Palwaukee Airport near where I live. I told him, 'Oh, gosh, Jack, I've got a family, and I've got this new job as president. I've just got so much on my hands.' He said he understood and asked if I would mind if he stopped by some other time. And I said no, that would be fine.

"Two weeks later, 'Captain Starr's here again.' I thought, My God, doesn't this guy get the message? Again I told him I just couldn't afford the time, but I really wanted to do it *someday*. Again he asked if he could stop back some other time, and I said, 'Fine, fine.'

"Two weeks later—guess what?" Dick laughs. "In walked Jack again. This is really a persistent guy, I thought, and I was all ready to start explaining again. But he just said, 'I know you haven't got the time, but I just wanted to drop these books off. If you get time, read them.' Then he left.

"Not long after that, I was flying across the country with Eddie Carlson, and I started reading one of the books Jack had given me. Eddie saw the book, and asked, 'What are you doing?' I told him reading a book on flying. Well, he said, 'You can't do that! You haven't got the time! You have responsibilities! You have obligations!' To show you the kind of relationship we have, I just smiled and didn't say a word, but I thought to myself, That does it. He can't tell me I shouldn't fly. I'm going to learn how.

"Then I just waited, and it wasn't a week later until Jack Starr came into my office again. Before he could open his mouth, I said, 'Don't say anything. I'll tell you what. The only time I have is Sunday morning at seven.'

"So Jack started giving me lessons every week. Well, I've got to give him all the credit. For two years he worked his schedule as a captain around my travel schedule; and if we ever went to a city where it was convenient for me to fly privately, we'd do that. First we rented a Cessna 172, and then a multiengine Cessna 310, and then I transitioned to the jet. I've got about six hundred hours today, about five hundred of them in a Lear. And it's all due to Jack Starr.

"Now here's the best part." Dick beams with the recollection. "After I had soloed and had my multiengine rating, I couldn't wait to break the news to Eddie. I'll never forget it. We were sitting around a campfire one night at Bohemian Grove, and I was feeling pretty good. I said, 'Eddie, there have never been any secrets between us,' and then I told him about my flying, how I had soloed and done everything I had to do to get my license. 'But you don't have to worry,' I explained, 'because I'll never be in a plane again by myself. There'll always be someone in the right seat. I decided to do it, Eddie, to get a better understanding of this airline.'

"Eddie turned to me and smiled. 'Well, Dick, I'm glad you told me. I've been following your progress with great interest.' It turned out that when I had asked Bill Dunkle, our head of flight operations, to check out Jack's qualifications (which were excellent), I had never told Bill to keep it to himself. So he had mentioned it to Eddie, and had kept him posted all along!"

Dick is the only CEO of United who has ever flown a plane. While he is quick to admit that he is not an expert on flying, he does believe piloting helps him understand the business more thoroughly. "Pilots and mechanics are very, very important to the airline," he says, "and I feel I have a better rapport with them because I fly. When I talk to a mechanic, I can speak halfway intelligently about what he's doing to the airplane."

Nothing could better illustrate Dick's management style than this anecdote. He talks to United employees whenever he has a chance, and maintains an open door to anyone who wants to talk to him. He stresses that this is a UAL management philosophy that he himself learned from Eddie Carlson. "This *is* a people business," he points out. "And we find time to communicate with our people. We *make* time to interact with them. If Eddie had not taught me to be approachable, I wonder if Jack Starr would have ever felt comfortable coming to my office? And if he hadn't, I'm sure I would never have learned how to fly."

UAL, Inc., is a very large business, with more than 70,000 employees, and Dick points out that this can present a communication problem. "With an organization the size of ours," he explains, "the successive layers of management tend to act as filters, both up and down. It's not intentional, there's no malice to it, that's just the way it is with big corporations. And as the chief executive officer, it's likely that I'll hear the things I want to hear, or I'll say what I thought I heard, because in the translation things often come out differently. So I think it's vital that I have channels of communication open to all levels of the organization. Naturally, I see our thirteen senior officers, but it's also important for me to communicate with the other officers, the directors, the managers, the supervisors—*all of our people.* And the only way I can do that is get out there and spend time on the stump, much like a politician."

One result of Dick's "stumping" is that he is not in awe of the annual meeting, for which many CEO's spend a great deal of time preparing. "I've just never felt that way," he says, shaking his head. "Maybe I shouldn't say this, because it might bring bad luck, but a shareholders' meeting is a piece of cake for me. And that's because I meet with our people frequently all year round, and no one—I mean *no one*—asks more difficult and probing questions than your own employees."

While these rap sessions are demanding, Dick is characteristically enthusiastic about them. "I'll be at O'Hare," he says, "and within thirty minutes I'll draw a huge crowd. I've been in rooms surrounded by a hundred pilots. I don't make speeches. I just start off with 'Anybody got any questions?' And then I encourage them, because sometimes they'll just stand there in awe. Although," he adds with a grin, "occasionally I'll get someone who says, 'Are you sure you know what you're doing, Prez?' If nobody starts out with questions, I'll refer to the fact that we're changing the structure of the airline just now, and say, 'You know, I bet there are one or two of you out there who would like to ask what the heck's going on with this airline.'

"Well, I can't overemphasize the importance of the feedback I get in these sessions. Now, I don't mean to circumvent our management or break the chain of command, but a chief executive has to have his antennae out and be aware of the rough spots and problems. Then when you sit at the highest councils of a company like ours with its tens of thousands of employees, and there are a dozen or so executives around the policy committee table, you have a little better insight into what's going on. And I'll tell you something: In my opinion, it pays off in spades.

"The fascinating thing about it," he adds, "is that whether I'm talking to officers or pilots or flight attendants or anybody else in this company, the vast majority of the questions—I'd say 90 percent—are the same. That's because they all have the same concern about their company. And you only find this out by talking to people. It can't be done any other way. Sure, you can communicate in writing, but nothing, absolutely nothing, replaces the human contact. So we're constantly stressing that our senior officers should seek face-to-face contact."

Recently United undertook a massive effort to communicate with its people. Since the industry as a whole had been going through some difficulties, the officers believed that communication and feedback were more vital than ever. Consequently, seven senior officers conducted face-to-face ninety-minute rap sessions with various groups of managers throughout the United organization. "Within three weeks," Dick says with obvious satisfaction, "we were able to meet with over 90 percent of our seven thousand management employees. And you can't beat that kind of communication. Nothing can replace the fact that 'the boss comes out to see us!' "

Dick firmly believes that listening is at least as important in the communication process as talking. "It's vital to make certain that everybody has heard the same thing," he says, "and that everybody understands the same objectives and is moving in the same direction. But that can be very difficult to achieve. A number of recent studies have shown how little people actually *listen*. I'm constantly trying to learn to be a better listener."

Since the decision-making process at UAL, Inc., is consultative, Dick's listening skills are essential. "I don't believe in dealing with issues of far-reaching significance by talking to people on a one-to-one basis," he explains. "For example, instead of just talking to our head of finance about an idea, I may also bring our marketing and operations people into the meeting. This way, we establish an information center, and the idea goes through a complete review process. We try to examine the subject from every angle and get the best opinions available. That way, we can make the best possible decision. After we go through this process, when it comes to the corporate policy meeting we'll very often be in complete agreement as to the best course."

A further part of the communication process that Dick stresses is letting people know *why the decision was made*. "You have to be prepared to explain your decision so people can understand it," he states earnestly as he clasps his hands on his desk. "Then they'll say, 'Okay, I don't agree with him, but I understand why he did it.' At least they can see that you've used logic, and the decision wasn't just off the wall.

Sure, they might not buy your decision, you might not win converts, but they'll respect your reasoning. What if your decision still turns out to be wrong? Well, let's face it, everyone makes mistakes. When you do, you have to have the guts to admit you were wrong. I know this isn't original, but it's true that the only people who don't make mistakes are those who never attempt anything. So don't be afraid to make mistakes. Just don't make the same mistake twice!"

Decisiveness is a Ferris trademark. After becoming United's president in 1974, he soon became the industry spokesman in the battle to end government control of airline routes and fares. When Congress passed a law terminating the power of the Civil Aeronautics Board by 1985, Dick declared happily, "Deregulation will be the greatest thing to happen to the airlines since the jet engine."

Prior to deregulation, he points out, the airline industry was able to compete only in frivolous ways, through such amenities as food services and movies. "But we couldn't enter into real competition, pitting our resources against the market. And we couldn't make basic decisions a business should make, decisions about asset allocation, for instance. Those decisions were made by the federal government, and the government cannot make those decisions efficiently or effectively—not the way market-oriented management can. It's true that there's a public utility aspect to our business. But the fact is that in a free and competitive market-oriented system, we can operate more effectively and serve the public better.

"You can see this already," the youthful executive continues, "as United is withdrawing service from some small cities. Our smallest plane is a 737 with 103 seats. If we fly the 737 on a 500-mile segment as against a 200-mile segment, it's 28 percent more fuel efficient. With that, and our size and structure, we're geared for the long haul. A smaller airline can serve short routes from Fort Wayne, to name a typical small city, far more efficiently. In that instance, commuter airlines are now using a 50-seat deHavilland Dash-7. And they can actually serve the community better, with more flights each day."

Another aspect of regulation the airline industry fought was government control of fares. "It wasn't the lack of passenger service that killed the railroad business," Dick says, shaking his head. "What caused the demise of the New York Central and Pennsylvania was the Interstate Commerce Commission. They forced the railroads to serve points it was not economically sound to serve—the buyers were not sufficient. *And,* the railroads were not allowed to charge compensatory rates. What could they do? They kept on operating and living off their own depreciation and slowly starved themselves to death. They went bankrupt. I blame nobody but the ICC for that."

With an emphatic gesture, he asserts, "We looked at what the government had done to the railroad industry, and we said, 'We're next.' We knew we had to break away. In a free enterprise system, it's imperative that the competitive marketplace dictate. The government must give industry the freedom to conduct business without interference. Fortunately, the mood of the country was for that."

Dick believes it is appropriate for public utilities, such as the electric companies and the telephone system, to be regulated. "But if there are certain components of those systems that can be deregulated," he adds, "then in the long run it's better to deregulate them. Unless there is an absolutely essential reason to, government should not interfere with the workings of the marketplace. We're chartered by the *public,*" he explains. "All business is, and if we can perform a function more efficiently and more effectively than our competition, then we should be allowed to do it. And if we can't, we don't need the government to tell us that. Someone else will—a competitor! He'll come along and say, 'I can do that better,' and that's what keeps us on our toes.

"Why should any business be held back from competing?" he asks. "Now, I don't believe in growth for growth's sake. United is not on an ego trip to be the world's biggest airline. If somebody becomes bigger than us, I don't think it will bother me too much. What would bother me is if we were passed up because we were not serving a perceived need. But growth is a healthy thing. I don't think an industry needs a mandate to become bigger. A company earns its size by doing its job well. And if we are doing our job well, why should the public be deprived of our efficiency? Now if a company became so dominant that it squeezed out all competition and was like a government itself, then it might be necessary for the government to step in."

Whether Dick is talking about government regulation, developing a new luxury hotel, or piloting a plane, his enthusiasm is always contagious. He is so charismatic that after an impromptu rap session with United employees at a terminal it is not uncommon for someone to ask, "When are you going to run for President? Because I'll be your campaign manager!"

"Whatever you do," he says, "I think it should be done with energy and commitment. And above all, with enthusiasm. And in a management position, if you can convey your enthusiasm to other people, that's half the battle. If they can see that you're enthused, then they're going to feel the same way."

The young person who can demonstrate enthusiasm for his job, Dick believes, is the one who will go far. "It's important to have long-term goals," he says, "but what you want to concentrate on day by day is doing the job at hand to the best of your ability. Do it well, do it better than anyone else around you, and you don't have to worry about a thing. You'll stand out like a sore thumb, and pretty soon you'll be singled out for promotion. Because every company needs good people, so it's very easy to be recognized. Even in a large company like this one, the people who do well always stand out—and somebody is going to recognize them."

His own commitment to his job is such that he spends as much as 60 percent of his weekday time traveling. "I'll do anything Monday through Friday," he says. "I'll work eighteen hours a day. But the weekends belong to my family." Most executives in a position like Dick's are older than he is, and their families are grown. With sons aged eleven, fourteen, and sixteen, the young chairman feels a desire and a responsibility to preserve some time strictly for family.

At forty-five, Dick could conceivably be UAL's chief executive officer for the next twenty years. When asked if he thinks he will be, he smiles and replies, "Gosh, there's so much going on in the more immediate future. . . . We've broken the airline into its component parts, for instance, to allow each division to operate as a separate entity. This has never been done in a transportation company before. We're in the process of creating an entrepreneurial spirit. As you can see, we're doing a lot of exciting things around here.

"Then there's the regulatory reform we fought so hard for. Between now and 1985, when the CAB goes out of existence, there's a lot of work to be done so that this will be a healthy industry. I want to see us through this transition period, and I want to see our company earning consistent, reasonable profits year in and year out. I want to give our shareholders a reasonable return. I think all that can be done.

"That's a tall order. When that task is done successfully, then and only then will I contemplate the future."

4

Reginald H. Jones

CHAIRMAN OF THE BOARD AND CHIEF EXECUTIVE
OFFICER,
GENERAL ELECTRIC COMPANY

Reginald H. Jones joined General Electric's Business Training Course in 1939 as a clerical worker, and two years later became a traveling auditor. In 1953, after serving in two financial management positions, Reg assumed his first general management post in the company's apparatus area. In 1956, he was promoted to general manager of the Air Conditioning Division, and in 1958 became general manager of the General Electric Supply Company Division. When the Construction Industries Division was formed in January 1964, he was made its general manager. He continued to head both divisions until he was promoted to the position of group vice president of the Components and Construction Materials Group in 1967. On May 1, 1968, he was named vice president of finance.

Reg was elected a senior vice president two years later, and became a member of the Board of Directors on August 1, 1971. On March 1, 1972, he was named vice chairman of the board and member of the Corporate Executive Office. He was elected president of the company on June 23, 1972, and became chairman in December of the same year.

He is chairman of the Business Council and co-chairman of the Business Roundtable. In May 1979, President Carter named him as chairman of the President's Export Council. He is a member of the President's Advisory Committee for International Monetary Reform, and serves on the Board of Directors of Federated Department Stores, Inc. A trustee of the University of Pennsylvania, he is also chairman of the Board of Overseers of the Wharton School, and an active layman in the Congregational Church.

Reg was born in Stoke-on-Trent, England, on July 11, 1917, and came to the United States at the age of eight. He graduated from the Wharton School of the University of Pennsylvania in 1939. He and his wife, Grace, live in Greenwich, Connecticut. They have a son, Keith, and a daughter, Grace Vineyard. All are graduates of the University of Pennsylvania.

In a recent *U.S. News & World Report* survey, 1,429 American leaders named Reginald Jones the most influential businessperson in the United States. Undoubtedly, the fact that he is chief executive officer of General Electric, a global multi-industry company which grossed nearly $25 billion in 1980, had a lot to do with their choice. However, his acknowledged role as the spokesman of American business is also due to his positions as chairman of the Business Council and co-chairman of the Business Roundtable. In these capacities, he works with the nation's leading businesspersons as well as top government officials, up to and including the President of the United States.

"The Business Council," the distinguished-looking chief executive officer explains, "is an advisory group comprised of the CEOs of the country's leading corporations. We meet four times a year and are addressed by top government people— cabinet members, leading legislators, the President himself— and by thought leaders from other fields, such as academia. The dialogue that takes place at these meetings will hopefully be helpful both to members of the council and to those who address us. We seek to gain an understanding of the objectives and programs of government officials. Then we react to those and give counsel and guidance reflecting our business experience."

Reg goes on to note that members of the council are representative of American business, both geographically and by type of business activity. While active membership is limited to five years, CEOs who continue to serve in that capacity for their companies for a longer period may become graduate members. The meetings are usually attended by about 150 active, graduate, and honorary members.

The Business Council was founded in 1933 at the suggestion of Franklin Roosevelt's first Secretary of Commerce, Daniel C. Roper, to serve as a conduit between business and the New Deal administration. Roosevelt, however, showed little disposition to call upon the council; and council members looked with disfavor upon many New Deal policies and acts. During World War II, a closer relationship was forged as the council helped mobilize the U.S. economy for war. From this ready-made reservoir of managerial talent, many high positions in various government agencies were filled.

When Dwight Eisenhower became President, the council really came into its own. The first Republican President in twenty years tapped four council members for top posts in his administration. During the Kennedy years, however, the cozy relationship between the council and the White House came to an abrupt end. Secretary of Commerce Luther Hodges insisted that all council meetings where government officials spoke should be open to the press, and he further directed the council to take in small-business representatives.

The council then severed relations with the Commerce Department and became independent, declaring itself ready to advise not only Commerce but "all areas of government requesting its services." Liaison committees were set up with major federal departments—Treasury, Labor, State, Defense, and Commerce—and with the Council of Economic Advisers and the White House itself. When Lyndon Johnson took office, a new era of good relations between the administration and the Business Council was launched.

REGINALD H. JONES

In addition to his two-year assignment as chairman of the council, Reg was for six years (1974–80) co-chairman of the Business Roundtable, under the chairmanships of John Harper of Alcoa, Irving Shapiro of Du Pont, and Thomas Murphy of General Motors. These men were quickly identified as a new kind of business executive, clues to the future of the corporation.

"While the Business Council is an advisory group," Reg explains, "the Business Roundtable actually develops position papers on significant issues—taxation, inflation, energy, welfare, social security, many areas of public policy. These position papers are distributed to the legislative and executive branches of the federal government. And the CEOs who work on the papers are frequently called on to testify before Congress and explain the Business Roundtable's position in detail or to discuss the papers with economic spokesmen for the administration."

The lean, immaculately dressed executive emphasizes that the Business Roundtable does not concern itself with special interests. "The position papers it develops are of broad national concern," he says, "and they are in the broad national interest; they are not attempts to claim some particular benefits for industry."

The Business Roundtable has approximately two hundred member companies (including all those represented in this book). The criteria for membership are that the company be significant in terms of size and employment, and that the CEO be willing to involve himself actively in public policy formation. "He must not only participate in the development of these positions," Reg says, gesturing with a cigarette, "but he must also personally promote them in Washington."

The Policy Committee consists of about forty members, all CEOs, who meet six times a year in New York to discuss these position papers and then send them out to the membership. The full membership meets annually in June. In addition, many task forces meet independently and frequently to develop position papers for presentation to the Policy Committee.

A CEO who is active in one or both of these organizations will spend a significant percentage of his time dealing with what Reg refers to as "the externalities." Nevertheless, membership in the Business Council and the Business Roundtable is keenly sought. "The reason is very simple," Reg says. "The decisions made in the external area, particularly in government, can have more impact on a corporation than decisions made in a board room. They have such sweeping consequences that we must devote our time to this area to be sure that the impact of decisions made elsewhere is understood in terms of the results it will produce in the private sector.

"I believe that executives of the future will have to be as comfortable swimming in these societal waters as their predecessors were in the functional disciplines of marketing, manufacturing, engineering, finance, and so forth," he emphasizes. "I say that because I feel we have reached such a state in our mixed economy in this country that we no longer have a 'free' enterprise system. You've got to pay attention to what's happening outside the corporation, because the impact of those outside decisions is so great. The executives of the future are going to have long antennae, thin skins, and an ear to the ground. They will need to be very perceptive, so that they can forecast changes in public and governmental attitudes, and can operate in an anticipatory rather than a reactive mode."

Lighting another cigarette, Reg points out the difference between the executive of today and the executive of yesterday in terms of dealing with public policy. "There is a decided shift from what some call the Neanderthal type of business executive who was just 'agin' whatever happened. In other words, he was presented with a piece of legislation, and he flew off the handle and shouted, 'This is going to destroy America!' Today, on the other hand, executives recognize that there are interests other than business, and we try to find areas for discussion, evaluation, and compromise. The executive who excels in the business disciplines today is willing to spend the time required to understand public policy, to do the reading, to talk with a variety of publics, to develop the necessary empathy with the politician.

"The politician has a very difficult role, you know," Reg continues. "In today's highly politicized economy, he is beset with demands from such a wide variety of special interest groups, on such a variety of issues, that he welcomes someone who comes to him with a relatively objective point of view."

Another change Reg has seen during his four decades with General Electric is in the relationship of business to the press. Referring to the time when many businessmen were reluctant to appear in public forums, he comments, "They felt that in the private sector they had the right to remain private. However, when it became evident that the public sector had invaded their domain, they realized it was time to speak out. I think it's fair to say that the current crop of leading businessmen have become open to the media. They appear on television programs, they hold considerably more press conferences. They're willing to subject themselves to all kinds of questioning, because they feel strongly that the business point of view on an issue should be put forth."

Reg, who has been willing over the years to speak out on public issues, is pleased with the new crop of executives who are following suit. He points out that this is necessary to counter the traditional anti–big business American attitude. "It's natural, I think," he says, "for an American to always have some concern about bigness, whether it's big business, big government, or big labor. Americans root for the underdog—it's part of our culture. The only times big business has accepted have been times, as in World War II, when the need for production transcended all other considerations. In the halcyon days after the war, too—when there was rapid growth in the economy, and a steady rise in real incomes and in productivity—business was tolerated. But the minute that the economy begins to falter, the critics of big business generally find that they've got a pretty good following."

Picking up the pipe he smokes between cigarettes, Reg continues. "I think it's important for business to remain aware that its biggest asset is its public franchise; by that I mean *the right to exist.* The people of the United States must *want* a General Electric, a General Motors, an AT and T to continue, because they value the products and services the companies provide. I believe that a company's concern for its public franchise must transcend all other considerations.

"It is also true under our enterprise system," he says, "and I want to emphasize this point, that the freedom to fail exists, as well as the freedom to succeed. If you do not provide a product that the consumer considers a good value, you don't last very long. Look at the turnover of the big companies in the United States, which is far greater than most people think."

In view of this philosophy, Reg believes it is wrong for the government to subsidize a company that is failing. He cites Chrysler Corporation as an example. "Of course the large number of Chrysler employees is a prime concern," he says. "But we have a mechanism in this country—the bankruptcy mechanism—which would probably result in a reorganization of that company. Certain significant and profitable parts of the corporation would continue; other parts would be acquired by other companies. Without question, the obsolete and low-productivity plants would be closed, and the employees in those particular plants would require retraining or perhaps relocation. But I want to stress that it would be a lot cheaper for the United States to take care of these pockets of unemployment on a direct basis than to try to maintain the total structure of Chrysler. I would rather the government provide for the individuals than try to take care of the companies.

"Where do you draw the line?" he asks, raising his eyebrows. "If you go to the aid of one, you open yourself up to going to the aid of all. It's a very dangerous precedent." He points out that GE testified publicly against the loan program to Lockheed several years ago, and that the company has not changed its position. "By aiding ailing companies," he adds, "we are picking up another one of the practices that the United Kingdom has found to be so unproductive. Just at the time when Mrs. Thatcher's government is moving to divest itself of business operations that have been acquired over the years, here we are in the United States talking about making the same kind of mistake."

During periods of economic stress, and particularly in inflationary times, the public attention is often drawn to the salaries of corporate executives. Reg believes the compensation of top executives must be seen in perspective. "If you compare the salaries of this country's corporate chiefs," he says, "with the earnings of the entertainment stars of America, you'll find the former pale by comparison. Again, many owners of private businesses make far more, particularly when you consider their opportunities in the area of capital gains, which are taxed less than the earned incomes of professional managers. Just recently, the fellow who runs the limousines between New Haven and the New York airports sold his business for about $13 million. That's pretty good compensation for developing a small business—and I say more power to him!

"But my concern is incentive, which is an essential factor in our system. I believe the worst thing a company can do is underpay its managers. When you do that, you end up with mediocre people, and that is no favor to the shareholders. If you cut the salaries of top management, you get into what I refer to as the danger of compression. There has to be a gap between the earnings of the CEO and the earnings of those next in line; then there has to be another gap, and so on. If you don't pay the CEO adequately, you end up with this compression down the line. And the company won't be able to attract good middle and upper management, because it won't be able to pay competitive salaries."

It can also be argued that high salaries may lead to a level of affluence that might adversely affect motivation. Reg admits that in some cases that could happen. "But fortunately," he says, smiling, "it's been my experience that there are always enough young tigers out there who want to show their mettle."

Reg was a young tiger when he joined General Electric in 1939 at the age of twenty-two. He began by doing clerical work, and after two years became a traveling auditor. His experience auditing a diverse array of company businesses, ranging from light consumer goods to heavy apparatus, has been especially useful. He points out, however, that it is not necessary to be in finance to have broad experience. GE's technical people, who come into the company in various training programs, also get the chance to work in different businesses within the company organization. "It's not just the area in which you enter the company," he says, "but the effort you're willing to put forth. Whatever your field, it's that extra effort that you put into the learning process which presents opportunities for advancement."

"The *sine qua non* of success," Reg states, "is on-the-job training. You learn a great deal in the school of hard knocks. But I have been able to combine that practical experience with numerous courses given by General Electric. I was in the first advanced management course at Crotonville, a thirteen-week program. And I've had many other company courses which have been very helpful."

After his work as a traveling auditor, Reg held two positions in financial management. Then in 1953, he was given his first general management position, within the apparatus area of the company. In 1956, he was promoted to operating a division in the consumer goods area, and two years later was named general manager of the General Electric Supply Company Division, the distributing arm for many of the company's products. In 1964, he also assumed command of the Construction Industries Division. He went to New York as a group vice president of the Components and Construction Materials Group in 1967.

The following year, he was promoted to vice president of finance, a position he almost refused because he enjoyed operations so much. "You have to really enjoy a job to be successful at it," he stresses. "And after fifteen years in general management, I wasn't particularly interested in returning to finance. But the job of vice president of finance was very challenging. It was the first time the company had combined the functions of the vice president comptroller and the vice president treasurer. Once I took the job and committed myself to it, I enjoyed myself so much I didn't want to leave it either!"

Reg believes that the capacity to devote oneself to the job at hand is a vital ingredient to success. "I've seen it happen," he says, "where a person becomes so concerned about his *next* job that he's not putting real effort into his current job. If you get yourself involved in what you're doing, and if you're proficient at it, the next job takes care of itself. Certainly it's important to have long-term goals; but they are best achieved by concentrating on the job at hand."

Always totally committed to his own work, Reg still puts in long hours in his position as CEO. His day begins at seven-fifteen in the morning when he arrives at his spacious office in Fairfield, Connecticut. He is usually in the office until after six at night, unless a business meeting or dinner is on the agenda. Since the "black tie circle" in New York City often requires his presence, he lives in Greenwich, Connecticut, a forty-five-minute drive from both Manhattan and Fairfield. Although he works a twelve-hour day, Reg also finds he often has to work Saturday and Sunday afternoons, and sometimes early Sunday evening. Saturday mornings he prefers to devote to golf or gardening, and Sunday morning to the Congregational Church, in which he is an active layman.

To Reg, his calendar does not seem overwhelmingly full. He looks at it serenely. Before April has ended, May is booked—with the exception of two Saturdays and Memorial Day—no appointments available. He cheerfully points out that in June, however, a few spots are still open. He shrugs. "I think this is fairly typical of what most CEOs are faced with."

Because GE is an international company, its CEO will allot time for foreign travel. In the first quarter of this year, Reg was in Brazil; in the second quarter he will go to Europe. The third quarter is blocked out for the Far East—Japan, Taiwan, Korea, and Australia. And in the fourth quarter he will spend a week in Europe again.

Once these major blocks of time are reserved, standing meetings are filled in. Every couple of weeks, Reg meets with the vice chairman; once a month he meets with the senior staff. In addition, there are periodic meetings with the sector executives and the vice chairman for strategic planning and budget review. In one month, the group may spend two full days in Session C, discussing and reviewing the progress of management talent. Like most other CEOs, Reg spends a major portion of his time in meetings.

Preparing for meetings accounts for another sizable chunk of schedule, and quiet time for reading and thinking can be difficult to come by. But Reg enjoys a reputation for being fully informed, whether he is meeting with senior staff or high government officials. "I think you'll find that successful CEOs are people who do their homework," he says with an eloquent gesture. "If you don't, your associates will know it. You can't go before your peers and present yourself as an omniscient seer. You either know what you're talking about or you don't, and you can't fool them. But you also wouldn't want to let them down. It's your own pride in the organization and your own need for peer approval that makes you find that extra time and put in that extra effort."

Recently, at a dinner in St. Louis, Reg found himself with several other CEOs discussing the qualifications they looked for in a successor. "We went through the usual list." He smiles. "Intelligence, integrity, character, personality, and so on. Then somebody mentioned energy, and everyone agreed 'That's vital!' And it is. If you didn't have a high energy level, I don't know how you'd get this job done."

Reg, who works at a pace that would exhaust most people half his age, is modest about his own energy. "Health," he notes, "you must be blessed with good health. And then, if you've got the enthusiasm and interest, it's amazing how you generate your own adrenaline. You just drive ahead."

Like most busy people, Reg is an expert at finding time. "Time management is of the essence," he states, pointing to a stack of files and reading material piled neatly on the right-hand side of his desk. "I find that I have a fair amount of time to read in the back of the car and on planes."

But the secret of finding the time and energy to handle his job as CEO as well as his demanding outside activities seems to lie in his attitude. "Oh, yes," he says, his eyes lighting up, "I do enjoy my work. I'm quite sure I wouldn't have the energy level or devote the amount of time I do if I wasn't enjoying it. My work is very challenging and highly rewarding. And I get to work with the greatest group of people. That's the thing! The General Electric family has a culture all its own. We're really concerned about each other—interested in each other. The support of these tremendously talented people just drives me on. It lifts my energy level, my enthusiasm, my interest—and I think most of us here feel that way."

Like all other CEOs, Reg spends a major amount of his time with people. "In a position like this, you realize very quickly that as a result of your own efforts"—he gestures with his pipe—"your own *personal* efforts, very little can be done. Everything that is really of consequence is done through people. You must get the support of the organization. And you can only do that if they understand your objectives—if they've had an opportunity to discuss their views with you and argue it through. Then we can arrive at a solution and say, 'By gosh, yes, this is the way we want to do it.' So a very large portion of my day is devoted to discussions with people— both inside and outside, by telephone, through correspondence, in person—constant communication."

One group with which Reg maintains that constant communication is GE's senior executives. The company has about forty strategic business units. Prior to introducing sector management, in-depth planning required that Reg and GE's three vice chairmen analyze in depth detailed strategic plans for each of these units. But the demands on the time of these executives were such that Reg did not feel they could give this planning the conscientious study warranted. In 1976, Reg introduced sector management, whereby each of six executives runs a multibillion-dollar product area. The sectors are: Consumer Products and Services, Industrial Products and Components, Power Systems, Technical Systems and Materials,

International, and Utah International. The last, Utah International, was a $2.2 billion acquisition, the largest merger in American history when Reg engineered it in 1976.

Sector management has worked extremely well for GE. "In the consumer area, for instance," Reg says, "we were able to develop synergies and harmonies when we looked at the strategic business plans of the various businesses that were serving the general consumer in the United States and around the world. We found tremendous opportunities to coordinate the strategic plans of these various businesses and produce economies for us. There is certainly a more rapid transferral of good ideas among the units. A sector executive, having done that kind of job, could now develop a strategic plan for all the consumer areas of the company. And we in the Corporate Executive Office could devote our time to looking at six plans for the six sectors, and to coordinating those six into a meaningful corporate plan. Sector management has been very helpful and productive for us."

In many large companies, separate corporate structures function within the company as individual entities; GE, however, operates as a single entity. Such departments as Corporate Research and Development and Corporate Production and Operating Services work together instead of individually, as would companies under the umbrella of a conglomerate. "We're able to draw from the inputs of all these units," Reg explains, "and thereby enhance the results. And the whole is greater than the sum of the parts. If we had separate corporate structures working as a loosely knit group, in my opinion we in the Corporate Executive Office would simply be portfolio managers. And I think we would not be doing the best job for our shareholders. We believe a much better job is done when we're all part of the same family, and we have this very, very close coordination and cooperation among the units."

While much of Reg's time is spent working closely with the sector managers and other top executives at GE, he also follows the careers of key people closely and personally. Files behind his desk hold personnel folders that detail the jobs, the educational backgrounds, and the compensation of people in GE's vast management network. Photographs in the files help Reg visualize a person and remember any discussions they've had together.

Beyond this, in his long career he has come to know several thousand GE employees on a first-name basis. "I've been to many, many of our operations," he says with pride, "and I've kept in touch with quite a few people and personally followed their careers."

Reg is convinced that remembering people by name is well worth the effort, and he illustrates this principle with an anecdote. Recently, visiting a foreign operation, a manager came up to him and apologized.

"So I asked him, 'Why?' " Reg recounts.

"He said, 'Well, about five years ago you went through an operation I was heading and asked me a question. And I gave you the wrong answer. You knew it—I could tell by the look on your face and a very indirect comment you made about half an hour later—but you never said anything. I went back and checked the facts, and I had made a mistake. Well, I want to apologize.'

"I did not remember that incident," Reg concludes, "although I remembered the individual. But *he* remembered—that's the point. These personal contacts are important. That incident had preyed on his mind for five years, until he could personally discuss it with me. I think it shows that time spent with our people is well spent, because it means a great deal to them."

Reg Jones, who is decisive, elegant, and dignified, is also described by GE people as sensitive and human; and the affection the GE family has for him is obvious. "He's quick to praise and hand out credit," one executive says. "He'll always say, 'I don't do it all by myself.' "

Another confirms this. A salesman in Atlanta says that Reg called him after a big sale just to tell him he was doing a fine job, and that the company appreciated it.

It is not difficult to find stories that demonstrate the warmth

Reg brings to his work. The man who polishes Reg's ideas for the many speeches he gives throughout the year comments that Reg always tells him how the speech went. "Some executives just take the work for granted," he says, "but Reg knows the importance of feedback. I not only learn how to do the work better, but also get a lift from the conversation. That's the kind of man he is; he doesn't want to let you down."

The warmth of Reg's concern extends beyond company business. When one executive was convalescing from heart surgery, he received several handwritten notes from Reg and then regular calls to see how he was getting along. And Reg's down-to-earth compassion was demonstrated when the minister of his church passed away. Reg made a point of discovering what he could do to really help. And that weekend he spent with the widow helping her fill out income tax forms.

When Reg was head of GE's wholesale distribution, the company honored one of its top salesmen at a banquet. As the salesman approached the dais to accept the award, Reg burst into enthusiastic applause. Later, a member of the audience commented on his obvious sincerity: "Who is that guy, your brother-in-law?"

"No," Reg said, "he's just GE."

Reg is quick to point out that his attitude is not unique. Like many others, he describes GE, a company of over 400,000 people, as having a distinctively warm atmosphere. "The General Electric culture is best exemplified by the concern we have for each other," he says. "Let's say one of our fellows has a problem—perhaps a serious illness or a death in the family. I will usually do what I can for the family. And here we think that is quite natural."

The GE spirit is evident when Reg talks about the biggest disappointment the company has suffered in recent years. In 1970, when Reg was financial vice president, GE decided to withdraw from the computer business. Although it had successfully ventured into aerospace and nuclear energy, the company suffered setbacks in computers. "We were not too happy about getting out of computers," Reg admits. "We have a great deal of pride. It was a very difficult decision. But nobody bats a thousand. In major league baseball, you're a star if you bat over three hundred. Nobody expects a man to get a hit every time he comes to bat, and this is also true of corporate executives and of corporations themselves."

With the matter-of-fact attitude that is so characteristic of him, he adds, "You can't be all things to all people. Even a company as great and as diversified as GE can't succeed in all businesses." Once the decision to get out of the computer field was made, Reg negotiated the sale of the controlling interest in the division to Honeywell, Inc. "It was a much better way of getting out of the business," he comments, "than just closing it down and eating the losses." In fact, Reg's work on that transaction was masterful and knowledgeable, and $240 million of the loss was recouped.

Behind the desk in his airy contemporary office, Reg appears relaxed and serene. The windows look out on the peaceful hills of the Connecticut countryside. On the wall opposite his desk are bookcases filled with books on sociology, philosophy, business, and history. One shelf holds lead toy soldiers that once belonged to Reg's son, a reminder of Reg's British heritage. The heavy double doors to the office are almost always open. Through them, an entrance hall lined with glass showcases leads to a reception area. In the showcases, GE products, models, and numerous awards serve as reminders of the General Electric tradition.

GE dates back to 1878, when Thomas Edison was researching the incandescent lamp, and the Edison Electric Light Company was founded to support his inventive genius. Since then GE's technological contributions to mankind in fields ranging from aerospace to X rays have been too numerous to list. When Project Apollo landed a man on the moon in 1969, thirty-seven GE operations and over six thousand employees had been involved in the program. Today, GE technology is at work in more than 140 countries. Examples range from power generation in Japan and d-c transmission in Zaire to locomotives for Latin America and jet engines for the A300

European Airbus. Some 15,000 technical-degree holders and 1,500 Ph.D.'s are employed by GE in research, development, and engineering.

Statistically, GE's record is undeniably impressive. Over the years, the company's engineers and scientists have been producing patentable inventions at the rate of nearly four every working day. In 1979, GE received its 50,000th patent. No other company in the world is even close to this figure. In addition, GE people have won countless honors, including Nobel prizes, the top citations of professional societies, and more Industrial Research awards for innovation than any other enterprise.

When he talks about research and development, Reg speaks from his roles both as GE's chairman and as a business leader. GE itself is unquestionably committed to R & D (research and development), and spent $1.4 billion in this area in 1979. Of that sum, $640 million was provided by the company and $800 million by the federal government, the Electric Power Research Institute, and others. Reg himself is deeply concerned about America's loss of technological pre-eminence. "In our own company," he says, "we're trying to develop a technological renaissance, building our competence in this very significant discipline. But this nation as a whole simply isn't keeping pace with other nations in R and D expenditures. At one time, expenditure for R and D was 3 percent of our gross national product; now it's dropped to about 2.2 percent—that is a reduction of 25 percent! As a result, foreigners are now receiving 37 percent of all U.S. patents, compared to 20 percent in 1960—another indication that America is falling behind in the race."

Reg believes this decline can be traced in part to our present tax structure, which is a barrier to capital formation. He points out that whether we compare present-day capital formation to our own past performance, to that of other countries, or to our future needs, the United States has not been investing enough of its output in new technology, new ventures, and new plants and equipment. As evidence of this, he cites the fact that during the 1970s the country's real gross national product rose at an average annual rate of 2.8 percent—down from 4 percent in the 1960s. The main reason was that, during the 1970s, productivity growth was less than half of what it was in the 1960s, and most of the increase in the GNP came from growth in the labor force. Demographics suggest that in the 1980s the labor force will grow more slowly. Thus, Reg points out, we must have increased investment in new technologies and new equipment. Otherwise, he believes, we will see a continued downward drift in our national economic growth rate, along with a decline in our national position, chronic unemployment, and chronic inflation.

This inflation Reg sees as a particularly dangerous threat, and he believes combating it will be made much more difficult by the fact that so many people today are receiving public funds. "I'm referring to actual payments to individuals," he says, "welfare, social security, government transfer payments, whatever. In the mid-1960s, 28 percent of the federal budget was taken up by such payments; last year it was over *50 percent.* In a period of about fifteen years, we've seen a 93 percent rise in these payments in constant dollars. We *must* hold down government expenditures if we're to cure inflation. The answer is not a balanced budget *per se.* You can balance the budget by increasing taxation; but we're already taxing our people too much."

Reg emphasizes that the government does not produce wealth—it only redistributes. "And," he adds, with an emphatic gesture, "through its own inefficiencies it takes out a big chunk in the process. If we are to have economic growth and rising real incomes, we must reduce the size of the public sector as a percentage of our GNP. This is the only way we will cure inflation—the *only* way.

"But there are so many mouths at the trough," he adds, with a concerned frown, "and so many people are indexed against the ravages of inflation. The unions have their COLA's (cost-of-living allowance). Retired people have indexed social security. The poor have their increases in welfare and the minimum wage. Consumers and businessmen are learning the trick of living in debt. Politicians may talk about fiscal restraint, but Congress is enjoying the secret windfall of unlegislated tax increases because of the bracket effect on individuals and the underdepreciation effect on business. Many farmers and businessmen advocate soft money, anxiously protecting their price supports and subsidies. With so much of the economy essentially indexed, the question arises: Does this nation really have the willpower and self-discipline needed to unwind inflation?"

Reg is convinced that Americans will not be willing to make the necessary sacrifices until they realize just what inflation is costing them. "We're taking a lower standard of living in this country without knowing it," he says, "Our real incomes have dropped over the past few years; and the sooner we realize that this is the price of inflation, the sooner we're going to see that we have to bite the bullet. We'll have to be willing to take a diminished standard of living for a few years. We'll have to make certain sacrifices by reducing the size of our government sector, by making the necessary investment in new facilities and equipment, by heightening expenditures in R and D—and then we'll realize an increase in productivity. And as productivity rises, inflation will drop, and we'll have a rise in our real standard of living."

He lights another cigarette, exhales slowly, and comments, "In socialism, the primary concern is the equal distribution of wealth; in capitalism, the primary concern has always been the production of wealth. I'm reminded of a statement made by President Kennedy: 'A rising tide lifts all boats.' If you don't *create* wealth, you have nothing to distribute. And it's a fact that the capitalistic economies have provided their people with greater real incomes than the socialistic economies. I believe that the production of wealth should be our real concern. The country has enough humanitarian interests to assure that we will have a reasonable distribution of wealth. But what I think has happened is that this inexorable growth of the public sector has induced a high inflation rate and accentuated a shift from production to consumption."

Although his concern for this issue goes very deep, Reg

speaks as always, evenly and moderately: "I think it's essential to realize that real profit is a continually contracting share of our GNP. Profit is the cost of staying in business; it is truly one of the costs of business. And the reason we are having inadequate reinvestment, lowered productivity, a loss of technological pre-eminence, is that we've had inadequate profits. The return has not been sufficient to attract investment."

Many Americans today marvel at the Japanese economy. Japan's government and business community tend to work harmoniously instead of in conflict, as often seems to be the case in the United States. "We do hear a lot about Japan, Inc.," Reg remarks. "But I think we have to realize that the Japanese society is quite unlike our own. It is a consensus society, which emphasizes compromise. The United States has always been an adversary, or advocacy, society—a drastic difference. I don't believe Japanese customs and practices would be acceptable to the American people. Now, it's certainly true that by working together the Japanese government and industry have made rapid strides, and I think we should seek that kind of cooperation here. But I don't see it happening in the same way it did in Japan, where, for example, government is directly involved in corporate planning. I don't believe American businessmen would be happy to see that."

The views of Reginald Jones, considered the most influential businessman in America, are cautiously optimistic. He believes there *are* solutions to the problems of the American economy, but that these solutions will take a great deal of self-discipline on the part of all Americans. He believes, too, that the business community has a responsibility to make itself clearly heard in Washington—not as just another special interest but as an enlightened spokesman for the broad national interest. In recent speeches to business groups around the country, Reg has urged others to become as involved as he is. He concluded a recent talk with a reference to the construction practices of ancient Rome.

"When the scaffolding was taken down from a completed arch, beneath it stood the Roman engineer. If, as a result of his incompetence, the arch came crashing down, he was the first to know. It is no wonder that so many Roman arches have survived for two thousand years.

"If the towering structure of the American economy is to last, then we, too, who are responsible for building it, must be willing to stand firm and defend it."

5

Ralph Lazarus

CHAIRMAN OF THE BOARD AND CHIEF EXECUTIVE OFFICER, FEDERATED DEPARTMENT STORES, INC.

The son of one of the first families of American retailing, Ralph Lazarus began working at the family store, the Lazarus department store in Columbus, Ohio, when he was a young boy. His first full-time job after graduating from Dartmouth in 1935 was as a piece goods salesman. The following year he sold furniture. In 1937, he became buyer of furniture and, in 1939, merchandise manager of home furnishings. He served during World War II from 1941 to 1943 in the Office of Price Administration with the War Production Board. Upon returning to Lazarus, he became assistant to the store's general merchandise manager. In 1944, he was the public relations director and, the next two years, basement merchandise manager. He was elected to the office of vice president in 1947 and became executive vice president in 1950.

Ralph was named executive vice president of the parent company, Federated Department Stores, Inc, in 1951 and held that position until he was named president in 1957. Ten years later, he succeeded his father, Fred Lazarus, Jr., as chairman and chief executive officer. He has been a member of the Board of Directors since 1951.

He is a member of the Board of Directors of Chase Manhattan Bank, N.A., Chase Manhattan Corporation, General Electric Company, and Scott Paper Company. He has received honorary degrees from the University of Miami, Suffolk University, Xavier University, and Dartmouth College. He is a member of Dartmouth's Board of Trustees. In 1974, he received the Gold Medal Award from the National Retail Merchants Association. The National Conference of Christians and Jews presented him with the Brotherhood Award in 1975.

Ralph has been very active in the local community since 1935, when he was a volunteer in the Columbus United Appeal, which his father helped found; and he is past chairman of Cincinnati United Appeal as well as the national United Way. Presently, he is an active member of the Cincinnati Business Committee, which he helped to establish and of which he was one of the first co-chairmen. He serves on the Dean's Advisory Committee of the University of Cincinnati Medical School, the Advisory Board of the Cincinnati Council on World Affairs, and the Board of Overseers of the Cincinnati Symphony. He is a past president of the Commercial Club of Cincinnati and a member of the Commonwealth Club.

On a national level, he is a member of the Business Roundtable, the Business Council, and the Council on Foreign Relations, Inc. He is also a member of the Board of Trustees of the Committee for Economic Development and the Executive Committee of the Rockefeller University Council. Among various other memberships are the President's Advisory Committee on Trade Negotiations, the Board of Directors of the National Committee on United States–China Relations, Inc., and the Business Committee of the Arts.

Ralph lives with his wife, Gladys, in Cincinnati, where they raised four children. They have three grandchildren.

Federated Department Stores, Inc., is a diversified retail business and the nation's largest operator of department stores, with 1980 net sales of $6 billion. The stores employ over 115,000 people in twenty-five states. Yet the company is unknown to the average American.

"Federated?" a shopper in New York City might say. "Never heard of them. But Bloomingdale's now, that's a department store!"

Likewise, Brooklyn shoppers consider Abraham and Straus the place to go. In Boston, *the* store is Filene's. In Columbus and Indianapolis it's Lazarus. In Texas, Foley's and Sanger-Harris. In California, Bullock's and I. Magnin. In Cincinnati, Shillito's. In Atlanta, Rich's. In Florida, Burdine's.

In addition, the Federated family includes the Boston Store in Wisconsin, Levy's in Tucson, Goldsmith's in Memphis, and Rike's in Dayton. Ralph's, the California supermarket chain with ninety-five locations, is also part of the Federated empire. And so are mass merchandisers Gold Circle and Richway, and Gold Triangle, a Florida hard goods specialty store. All told, Federated includes 354 stores with more than 50 million square feet of retail space.

The twenty famous stores named here represent autonomous

divisions within the Federated family. Of these, none is more famous in its region than Lazarus, a $325 million business which has a customer loyalty in its area like few other U.S. stores. The Lazarus family, in fact, is often referred to as the first family in American retailing. The family's great retailing tradition began with Ralph Lazarus's great-grandfather, Simon Lazarus, who left Germany in 1848 to escape Jewish segregation laws and in 1851 set up a small men's clothing store in Columbus, Ohio.

The distinguished gray-haired chairman of Federated smiles as he recalls his own immersion in the family tradition as a youngster. "I don't know how young I began working in the store," he says. "I know one summer I was in men's handkerchiefs and I had to stand on a crate so I could see over the counter to wait on customers." He laughs, "But I loved it. I remember when I was twelve, how delighted I was to help the clerks unpack bedsheets. The sheets came in enormous boxes that were six feet deep. When the salespeople could no longer reach the sheets packed at the bottom, they held me by my heels and lowered me into the box. Then I would hand the sheets up one at a time. I would say that was one of my major contributions to the business."

Ralph literally grew up in the business, for even at home he was subject to the enthusiastic influence of his father, Fred Lazarus, Jr. "My father's whole life was built around the business," he recalls. "I remember his coming home in the evening just full of the store. It was the main topic of conversation at dinner. Even when I was a child, it was interesting, and over the years I naturally assumed I would go into the store also.

"During the summers, Dad felt that my three brothers, my sister, and I ought to be working if we weren't at camp or away on a trip. He didn't think we should be fooling around in country clubs. So I worked at the store." During these years, Ralph's father put him into different departments so that he could become familiar with as many facets of the business as possible and get to know the store personnel.

RALPH LAZARUS

Fabian Bachrach

While it is not uncommon for a young person to rebel against a family tradition, Ralph never felt pressured to become a retailer. "Any pressure I felt certainly did not come from the family," he explains. "It was self-imposed pressure. I always felt I had to do a better job than anyone else. And while my father and uncles might have set the pace, they didn't put pressure on me. I just assumed the business was going to be my career direction, and I was always enthusiastic about it."

Only once did Ralph entertain the idea that he might not work in the family business. At Dartmouth, he had roomed with the son of Morton May, the head of the May Company, who was a good friend of Ralph's father. After graduation, Ralph received an offer to work for the May Company. "I figured that it might be a good idea to get a track record somewhere else," he explains. "I told Dad, 'It might make things easier for you and me.' Well, Dad didn't think it was a very good idea at all, and I finally agreed with him. After I graduated, I started to work at the store full time on June 24, 1935. I happen to remember the date so well because it's also the date of my wedding anniversary." In his early years as a full-time retailer, Ralph sold everything from piece goods to furniture. He probably spent a longer period of time at a lower level in retailing than any other member of the family. "Sure, during the latter part of it, I occasionally felt some resentments," he admits. "But in the long run, that experience paid off."

Today, the Lazarus family retailing tradition continues with Ralph's thirty-four-year-old son, John, a branch store manager at Filene's in Boston. "John has an MBA," Ralph notes, "and he's been in the business nine years. Other than a couple of buying jobs in small departments, this is the first job he's had where he can really look at the bottom line and say, 'That's me!' "

Ralph is outspokenly proud of John. "Now, I haven't been out there since he became manager," Ralph says, "but from what I hear, he's steamed up the whole organization." He beams, and then grows thoughtful. "And let me tell you, there's pressure when you're the son of the chairman of the company you're working for. Everyone in the organization is watching you. I know, because I experienced it myself. I always felt I had to do at least 10 percent better than the next guy; and if a chairman's son doesn't, he's not going to be respected—and he's not going to be successful.

"I am also very proud of my son Jimmy, who decided to build his career outside of Federated and is doing exceedingly well. He is with Fieldcrest Mills."

A strong believer in practical experience, Ralph points out that on-the-job training may be more important in retail than in any other business. He adds, however, that it isn't possible today to attract bright young MBAs and expect them to spend as many years at lower levels as he himself spent. Management trainees at Federated go through a crash program, which Ralph describes as "a minimum." He explains: "We have to compress experience. It would be better if the training course lasted two or three years—but we just couldn't hold them."

Ralph is convinced of the importance of on-the-job training, because he has seen so many young executives fail not for lack of competence but because they have a "people blindness." Time after time, their inability to work with people traps them into making technically good decisions that just won't work in practice. "They haven't learned that an executive succeeds or fails not so much because of what he does," Ralph stresses, "but *because of what he is able to get someone else to accomplish.* Our business schools produce some highly qualified people, but many of them feel that their teachers have taught them everything they need to know. They believe their classroom training assures them success. They have the knowledge to make decisions which are technically correct, but they don't have the human sensibility to understand how to get people involved. Sensitivity to people is seldom developed under campus or laboratory conditions.

"Now, I don't mean to be repeating the old cliché about the difference between 'book learning' and 'practical experience.' And I don't want to go into the old story about learning the business from 'the bottom up.' But by my definition, practical experience means three things. First, it's a thorough understanding of how an organization works, what its principles are, and how and why they developed. Second, it's the knowledge of, and respect for, the people who were smart enough to come up with these principles and make them successful. And third, it's the realization that an individual can succeed in a particular organization only when he discovers how to contribute within the established framework—*and* only when he has learned that he is writing a song that someone else must sing.

"All this adds up to people experience," Ralph concludes slowly. "In other words, it's the development of antennae that will be sensitive to the intricate relationships of the modern corporation. This is where so many promising young people fall off the sled. Their educations have taught them how to come up with an abstract, academically correct answer. And once they do that, they think the job is done—never realizing that *what* you decide to do has to depend on *how* you plan to do it. Beyond that, you only know the *how* when you have visualized it in terms of the *who*. Good ideas are easier to come by than good implementation. A brilliant idea halfheartedly implemented is very likely to fail, whereas a mediocre idea carried out with passion and enthusiasm may succeed brilliantly. These polysyllables—'implement' and 'execute'—really mean *who* is going to do it, and *how* he will get it done."

His lifetime experience in the retail business has led Ralph to believe in the importance of a retailing executive trainee spending time in many different positions throughout a store. "It's terribly important to have been directly in touch with the salespeople and the rank and file personnel," he says. "That's the only way to learn what kind of people they are, how they react, what they believe in, what they object to, and so on." He pauses to sip his coffee and continues. "The reason this knowledge is so important is that every decision made at the top of the ladder relates to those people."

In addition to people knowledge, Ralph is a great believer in the importance of enthusiasm and conviction in management. "It's essential," he emphasizes, "that *whatever decisions you make, you make with conviction.* You're not going to be a dynamic leader if you can't do that. In this field, correct decisions have to be based on facts, but facts are not enough; you need spirit and soul. You won't be a real leader unless you fully believe your decisions will not only be acceptable but will be enthusiastically received by the thousands of people in the rank and file."

Putting down his coffee cup, Ralph clasps his hands and smiles. "I had my first lesson in the importance of enthusiasm many years ago, when I was a novice in the Columbus family store. We had a rug buyer at Lazarus, an old Englishman, who had gone down to market with a buying plan for the upcoming selling season. Well, he saw a job lot of Oriental rugs. They were old rugs and very fine, and this fellow knew quality when he saw it—and he bought them.

"Those rugs were totally beyond the historical means of that department. Oriental rugs had never been particularly popular in Columbus. At the time, my father was the general merchandising manager, and when he saw this—the biggest assortment of Oriental rugs any of us had ever laid eyes on— he just hit the ceiling!

"But that buyer stuck to his guns. He said, 'Listen, I *know* these rugs will sell, and sell well, and I'm going to sell them!'

"Dad was so angry he told the buyer, 'They'd better sell. Because if every one of those rugs isn't out of here in two weeks, you'd better get out!'

"Well, the rugs went out. Let me tell you, Columbus bought more Oriental rugs in those two weeks than it had consumed in the previous ten years! That's what conviction and enthusiasm will do.

"Now, I'm sure that if management had taken a survey of customers, it would have shown that my father was right. There was no burning desire on the part of Columbus consumers to carpet their floors with expensive Orientals. The prices were far beyond the department's normal range. There was no conceivable reason to put 75 percent of our floor-covering investment into a product Columbus obviously would not want. No reason, that is, except that the buyer's conviction and enthusiasm could translate that unsupportable idea into a cash-register success. Well, that's the kind of thing a retailer has to know."

Ralph points out that senior managers must also remain aware of the importance of enthusiasm among the rank and file. "A while ago, Federated management thought it would be appropriate to open a branch store in a particular division. The store management, however, really didn't want to expand, although they could see that a branch represented an excellent opportunity. We debated the question at length, and finally the store reluctantly agreed to build. The resulting branch was handsome in design, sound in policy, efficient in operation—and disappointing in results! It had everything going for it but the enthusiastic backing of the people who had to operate it. The 'right' decision had produced the wrong results. And *people were what made the difference.*"

He adds, "Now, I don't want to create the impression that I think a good executive accepts other people's ideas just because they happen to be enthusiastic about them. That would be nonsense. But it is equally true that you can't earn your keep in top management if all you do is bludgeon your subordinates into accepting your solutions. The best executive is a person who knows how to add human wisdom and effective salesmanship to the findings of the slide rule. It doesn't matter whether you're producing shoes or toothpaste or selling real estate or insurance; we're all in people businesses. We sell to people, we buy from people, and we look to people to implement our ideas."

Although there has been a trend in retailing toward self-service, Ralph insists that, in any retail operation, success still depends upon the rank and file employees. "Everything you do in a retail business comes down to people," he says. "Even in our supermarket chain, Ralph's, in California, we have found that while value is important to customers, they also want courtesy at the checkout counter. We think it's terribly important for managers to train our people to be customer conscious. If you go into a supermarket and receive a warm 'Hello, isn't it a nice day?' at the checkout counter, it makes a big difference. There again, people are what matters.''

Picking up a pencil, Ralph sketches on a legal pad. "Federated is really nothing but people. Look at the organizational structure here—what I call the upside-down chart. First, in each division we have a series of selling departments, where most of the contact with the customers takes place—women's lingerie, men's dress shirts, cooking utensils, and so on. In direct support of these selling departments are divisional merchandising managers and general merchandising managers. Next we have sales supporting departments that supply the merchandise departments with people and goods, and handle the accounting, personnel, and maintenance of the building. All of these people receive support from a two-man team of principals. One of these individuals is in charge of the sales supporting departments—operations—and the other is responsible for the merchandising area.

"It's very important that these two men complement one another; they don't just supplement one another in terms of strengths and weaknesses. They have to have a useful respect for each other, or it won't work out. It's a real team effort, and this is what runs each of our divisions. The top management must be effective in supporting the people at every level, and they must be able to recognize enthusiasm and be able to generate it. If they can't do this, I don't care how good the store's location is, or how beautiful the building is, it's simply not going to be a good store. As I keep saying, we're in a people business—and everything depends on the effectiveness of our people.''

The store principals in each Federated division are usually a chairman and a president. While one of them is identified as the chief executive officer, in the divisions which operate most effectively the CEO does not use his power to overrule

the other store principal. "That's how my father and I operated," Ralph says. "We weren't father and son—we were partners. I don't remember Dad's ever overriding one of my
decisions, and in turn I don't override decisions made by Howard Goldfeder, our president. I may disagree with him, and
I may try to convince him to do it another way; but never
do I interfere with his decision. And that's the way I worked
with our former president, Harold Krensky, as well.

"The system of having two bosses in each division, each
with enough authority to disagree with the other, has worked
out very nicely for us. In our business, improving the decision-
making process is always important. Most of our decisions
are made on a local level, and it's the nature of the retail
business that there are many more decisions to make on a
day-to-day basis than in, for instance, a manufacturing company. Often they're less weighty decisions. In manufacturing,
a decision on a product may involve millions of dollars, so
everybody right on up to the CEO will be in on it. But, with
the exception of a major decision such as building a new
branch, we are usually involved in thousands of day-to-day
decisions. So there is a constant effort on the part of store
principals, department managers, divisional managers, our
management at Federated—everyone—to get better decisions
made.

"And," he points out, "when you get down to it, our success
really depends on having a better batting average than the
competition. But often when a decision is wrong, if it's made
with enough conviction and carried out with enough enthusiasm you can make it work!"

The Federated philosophy of delegating decision-making and
encouraging divisional autonomy can be traced to the company's origins in 1929. (As Ralph comments with a chuckle,
"A good year to start a business, wasn't it?") At that time,
several of America's leading merchant families merged into
a loose holding company. At the founding date, November
25, 1929, they included the Lazarus family, who owned Lazarus and Shillito's in Ohio; the Filenes of Boston; and the Roth-

schilds, who owned Abraham and Straus in Brooklyn. Three months later the Bloomingdales of New York joined the corporation. Each store had been family-owned for several generations, but there were family members who were not active in the business. With the listing of Federated on the New York Stock Exchange at the time of the merger, those members who wanted to sell their shares were able to. From the beginning, the merger was harmonious, in part because the stores had all been members of the Associated Merchandising Corporation, a research and buying organization, where they had worked together and developed mutual respect.

For nearly two decades, Federated was a paper holding company for four largely autonomous family-run stores. It was not until 1945, when retail competition became tougher, that Ralph's father, Fred Lazarus, Jr., suggested Federated become a full-fledged operating company. The other merchants balked, but Fred was a dynamic individual. (Among his other accomplishments, he had helped persuade Franklin D. Roosevelt to change the date of Thanksgiving in order to have a longer selling period between Thanksgiving and Christmas.) He laid down an ultimatum: Do it his way, or he would pull Lazarus and Shillito's out of the company. When the others finally agreed to his proposal, Fred Jr. became Federated's CEO, and held the position until Ralph succeeded him in 1967. Initially, Fred Jr. worked from a small fifth-floor office above a Cincinnati bank. Today, Federated is headquartered in its own twenty-one-story office building in downtown Cincinnati.

Since it was a Lazarus who spearheaded the move to turn Federated into an active company, it's interesting that the headquarters were located in Cincinnati rather than Columbus. Ralph explains that his uncles, Simon and Robert Sr., along with their sons, Charles and Robert Jr., were all located in Columbus, and the family members had always worked as equals. "To headquarter Federated in Columbus would have set up an unequal situation," Ralph states. "Either Federated or the Lazarus name might have been overshadowed. My third uncle, Jeff, had been working at Shillito's, and Dad had been his supervisor, so there was no likelihood of animosity if Federated was located in Cincinnati. It just seemed the natural place to put it."

Despite the family retailing tradition, Ralph had no ambitions of heading Federated during his early career. "I did hope to run Lazarus someday," he says. "My father and his brother Simon were a two-man team, and I anticipated the same kind of arrangement with my cousin Chuck Lazarus, who is the chief executive officer at Lazarus now."

Ralph enjoys telling how his father and uncle used to run the Columbus department store. "They shared a single office, and they had their desks arranged so they sat back to back. They would hold conversations simultaneously with different people. And when they talked together, it was amazing. It sounded like one person talking, because one could start a sentence and the other would pick it up in the middle and finish it—they were so close and thought so much alike." It is believed that the concept of having two store principals was greatly influenced by the excellent working relationship of Fred Jr. and Simon Lazarus.

In 1951, Ralph was asked to move to Cincinnati and assume a major management role with Federated. It was a move he had never anticipated, and he admits that he did not leap to the opportunity. "As a matter of fact," he recalls, "my wife, Glad, and I took six months to make up our minds. We knew the job would require more travel, more time away from the family. We'd also have to move our children from their schools, and our daughter was just entering high school, which is an awkward age for a move. So we gave the relocation some very serious thought."

In terms of the position he would hold with Federated, Ralph, who was then thirty-eight, assumed that a more mature person would be put in the number-two spot. Since the Lazarus family was not Federated's principal stockholder, he did not expect a high office within Federated. "Then they began talking *president*," he says. "But the day before it was to come before the board, Walter Rothschild, chairman of the board's Executive Committee, asked me if we could keep it executive vice president. I didn't care about the title, and I thought it was a good idea, because Dad might have been reluctant to give up the title of president. And at that time there was no chairman. So I went in as executive vice president." In 1957, Ralph was named president, and his father became chairman. Ten years later, Ralph became CEO and chairman, and Fred Lazarus, Jr., was named chairman of the executive committee, a position he held until his death in 1973 at the age of eighty-eight.

People who have worked with Ralph describe him as thoughtful and gregarious; he enjoys needling close associates in a good-natured way. "He possesses an innate courtesy," says one executive. "That's a trait all the members of the Lazarus family seem to have." For all his pleasant nature, however, Ralph has some unshakable convictions about how Federated should be managed. He believes firmly in decentralized authority, with the power of decision placed as close to the customer as possible. Convinced that his job couldn't be done by sitting at his desk reading memoranda, he has spent most of his career at Federated visiting the divisions of the company.

There were years during his career when Ralph spent four days out of five in the field—seeing the stores, the merchandise, the customers, and the employees in their natural habitats. On these trips he would probe for information on which to base top management decisions. He looked for such facts as sales per square foot, gross margin, markups and markdowns, and all the other barometers of retail health. He also looked for intangibles.

During the time he directly supervised stores, he felt this experience was quite important. "I got three kinds of information out of store visits I could get no other way," he states deliberately. "First, I got what I call 'feel.' When you've walked through as many stores as I have, you can tell in a minute whether things are going well or poorly. A store that's on the move is like a happy child—delighted with life and full of the spirit of adventure. There's no way for anyone to conceal that ebullience, any more than a poorly run store can hide its dour salesclerks or its last-season merchandise.

"The second thing I gained from these visits is that I got to know the people. I've said this before: The difference between our store and the competition is whatever the people make it. Almost all the merchandise we sell can be found in competitive stores. We are a people business—and how we find our people, train them, handle them, and promote them will pretty much determine our future.

"Third, I visited stores because I wanted to find out not only what store management proposed to do, but how much conviction and enthusiasm they would bring to this task. I've also said this before, but it's vital: Even a questionable decision carried out with passion and enthusiasm can succeed brilliantly. I look for that enthusiasm."

Only once did Ralph visit a Federated store unannounced. "I was curious to see the reaction," he explains. "But it was instantly apparent that it wasn't a good idea. By surprising the store principals, I'd downgraded them. You must realize that these individuals are running an organization of a thousand people or more. They're leaders in their community, and they're looked up to both inside and outside the store. The situation is not the same as when the chairman of a large chain outfit like Sears drops in out of the sky and goes through one of his stores. Managers of chain stores are not at the same level as our store principals. They don't have the same authority and responsibility. So dropping in on a store for an inspection is something I have made a point of not doing again."

Working with twenty divisions created a hectic schedule for Ralph. There were semi-annual planning meetings at the Cincinnati headquarters with each divisional management team to discuss six-month plans. In addition, Ralph made periodic two- or three-day visits to each division, during which he discussed the stores' strengths and weaknesses with management. When there was a difference of opinion, Ralph would advise and counsel—never issue dictums.

During his visits, he carried a book with all important data about the store, information about organizational changes since his last visit, and key areas to be concentrated on for improvement. The book served as an outline and kept Ralph up to date. In addition, each store prepared a laundry list of things that were troublesome, which Ralph could observe and discuss with management. Store visits typically involved a series of conferences with many different people seeking solutions to specific problems. From the point of view of the store management, this guidance from someone with Ralph's experience and knowledge who was not involved in the day-to-day operation of the business was invaluable.

One of the aspects of these visits that Ralph enjoyed most was meeting the new people and chatting with them about their departments. As thousands of Federated people have discovered over the years, Ralph has an uncanny ability to remember names—even when talking to employees he hasn't seen for a year or longer.

Ralph's career has always required him to spend a great deal of his time traveling. During his early days at Lazarus, he made many buying trips, and often visited other stores within the Associated Merchandising group to pick up ideas and to learn why one store might be having unusual success in a particular area. "In those days I was never home on Monday nights," he recalls with a chuckle, "because that's the night we were open back then, and so were our competitors. So I went to check them out." There were also times during his career when Ralph had to travel for two or three weeks at a stretch. "But regardless of how far away I was," he says, "I made it a point to come home every weekend. It didn't matter if it meant going back out to the Coast on Sunday night—I was determined to be with my wife and children on weekends."

At the point in Ralph's career when it was obvious that traveling would seriously infringe on his time at home, he and his wife discussed the problem. One decision they made was to give up golf and instead take up tennis. A court was built at their home so the whole family could enjoy the game together. A second decision was to cut their social life down and reserve the weekends strictly for family. "The family is number one," Ralph says matter-of-factly. "I was brought up to believe that family came first, business second, community third, and the nation fourth." He pauses characteristically to think, and continues. "Those were the responsibilities you had, and that was the order of priority. I accepted it, and it's worked well for me. I think every family member of my generation feels about the same way I do. It's obvious that their commitment to their community has remained the same."

The Lazarus family's belief in community involvement has become a business philosophy shared by management throughout Federated's twenty divisions. "We run a business that's basically a corporate citizen," Ralph remarks. "We believe we should not only be generous financially but that our people should be generous with their time and make major commitments to the cultural, educational, and philanthropic institutions of the community. This is more than simply a public relations program with us. We serve our hometowns not only out of civic pride but out of necessity. If the community's educational programs, for example, go down the drain, it will no longer be an attractive place to live in. We won't have as many new customers or as many new businesses moving in. And retail stores are not in a position to pull up stakes and steal away to greener pastures when things go sour. Our present and future are tied to the streets where we live and where we have built our businesses. We want them to be healthy streets, safe streets, and happy streets—and we intend to do our part in making them that way."

Federated as a whole and the individual stores have been aggressive proponents of giving support to the community. People on every level are encouraged to be active in whatever interests them—church, school, Little League. "When we have men or women in management we think are real comers," Ralph states, "we like to see them put on some outside responsibilities, such as the United Appeal, the art gallery, or the symphony. We want to see what kind of influence these people can have in an area where they have no authority within the organization. It gives us a clue to the quality of their leadership.

"Furthermore, it broadens an individual's scope, which I think is very important. We don't want a person thinking twenty-four hours a day about how to sell men's underwear. We want a person with varied interests. So we'll give company time to the community, as well as expecting our people to use some of their off-time in these commitments. And do you know what? A good executive can find the time by organizing and delegating more authority to an assistant, and we don't have to worry about who's minding the store while that person is involved in the community."

Ralph's management style is clearly expressed in his office. Rather than a standard desk, he uses a round table with four chairs. "I have a phobia about sitting at the head of a table," he says with a slight shrug. "I don't like to feel superior to the next fellow—it makes me uncomfortable." He also mentions that he never has anything between his desk and the door to his office; he likes to be able to get up and greet a guest with no obstacles in the way. His closeness to his family is indicated by an oil painting of his father on the wall near the door, and photographs of his wife and children displayed around the room. Draperies, walls, and a matching chair are all covered in a quiet, elegant gray and green fabric. The large room includes a conference table with six chairs, and a conversational area with a sofa and chairs. With windows on three sides, the office overlooks the city of Cincinnati, the Ohio River, and the hills of Kentucky.

Headquartered in the heart of Cincinnati, Federated places a strong emphasis on the commitment of its stores to their downtown communities. "In most communities, downtown is the center of activity," Ralph explains, "both business activity and cultural events. So we have found that the downtown store sets the image of the total store more effectively than any branch. There are exceptions, of course. In Miami, a branch of Burdines does four times the volume of the downtown store, and in Los Angeles the downtown is not the magnet of the community. But in general, downtown stores like I. Magnin in San Francisco set the image for all the branches. And you know, even if it's less convenient, customers will come to the downtown store if it's the image store. They want to make their major purchases there—Christmas gifts or back-to-school shopping."

While each Federated store is known for its unique personality and style, the stores share a commitment to courtesy and special service. Over the years, this has developed customer loyalty that often passes down from one generation to another. "We attempt to offer such superior service," Ralph says, "that the customers will come to us when they have a need. For example, although most customers don't require delivery any more, we will deliver the merchandise if they request it—and promptly."

Another example of a special brand of service occurred at Lazarus in Columbus during the Depression. "We had thousands of customers who were paying us as little as a dollar a month," Ralph recalls. "We knew what kind of trouble they were having, and we felt the important thing was to maintain contact with them. We'll still work something out today for a customer who is having trouble paying his bills. Well, people remember things like that, and those Depression customers stayed loyal to us long after the thirties were over. Some of their children shop with us today."

However, Ralph points out, to retain a customer's loyalty, a store has to perform. "Today's customers shop more. They are much more price-conscious, and often they will visit several stores before making a buying decision. They're fashion-conscious, too. Customers won't take the store's word for it that this is the latest thing—they want to see what the competition has. Service alone is not enough. We have to offer good merchandise at competitive prices."

With this kind of emphasis on good value and good service, it's no wonder that the Federated stores enjoy the highest possible reputation in the retail community—as well as with millions of consumers. But Ralph issues a gentle reminder of a favorite saying within Federated: "In this business, today's peacock is tomorrow's feather duster." Like every other business, retail stores cannot afford to rest on their laurels. Ralph smiles. "It doesn't matter whether we're talking about people or merchandise or customer preferences, the one thing that's constant in the retail business is change. You simply can't afford to stand still. Things are going to change—that's inevitable."

Another inevitable change at Federated will occur when Ralph retires. When the subject is mentioned, he says, "There's a schedule we are working on."

Since Federated was founded in 1929, it has been headed by a Lazarus. When Ralph retires, it seems unlikely that another Lazarus will head the company. Ralph accepts this matter-of-factly. "Federated is a public company. We've shifted the business over the years from a family company to a professionally managed company. So my successor will probably not be named Lazarus. And I think that's the way it should be."

JERRY McAFEE

6

Jerry McAfee

CHAIRMAN OF THE BOARD AND CHIEF EXECUTIVE OFFICER, GULF OIL CORPORATION

Following in the footsteps of his father, who was employed at Gulf, Jerry McAfee joined the company at Port Arthur, Texas, in 1945 as a chemical engineer. In 1950, he was transferred to Gulf's Research and Development Center in Harmarville, Pennsylvania. He became vice president and associate director of research in 1954; a year later, he was appointed vice president of engineering in the Refining Department in Pittsburgh. In 1960, he was named executive technical adviser, and in 1962 he also undertook the direction of the Planning and Economics Department. Two years later, he was appointed senior vice president of Gulf Oil Corporation and Gulf Eastern Company in London, where he also served as a director of the Kuwait Oil Company and Iranian Oil Participants Limited. After moving to Canada in 1967, he became president of Gulf Oil Canada Limited in 1969, a position he held until 1976, when he was elected chairman and chief executive officer of Gulf Oil Corporation.

Jerry was born in 1916 in Port Arthur, and was raised in that Texas oil-refining city. He graduated from the University of Texas in 1937, having majored in chemical engineering, and he earned his doctorate in chemical engineering from the Massachusetts Institute of Technology in 1940. During World War II, he helped design and start aviation gasoline plants.

He serves on the boards of the Mellon Bank, the American Petroleum Institute, the Aspen Institute for Humanistic Studies, the M.I.T. Corporation, the Greater Pittsburgh Chamber of Commerce, the Pittsburgh Symphony Society, the World Affairs Council of Pittsburgh, the Regional Industrial Development Corporation of Southwestern Pennsylvania, and the Allegheny Conference on Community Development. He is a member of the National Petroleum Council, the National Academy of Engineering, the American Institute of Chemical Engineers, and the American Chemical Society. While living in Canada from 1967 through 1975, he actively participated in business and community affairs.

Over the years, Jerry has held prominent positions in a number of technical and petroleum-industry societies. After several years as a director of the American Institute of Chemical Engineers, he also served as their national president in 1960. He helped represent the United States on the Permanent Council of the World Petroleum Congress from 1955 to 1964; and from 1961 through 1963, he was a member of the Advisory Board of the American Chemical Society's Petroleum Research Fund. In 1963, he received a certificate of appreciation from the American Petroleum Institute's Division of Refining for his work in air and water conservation. He was elected a member of the National Academy of Engineering in 1967.

He and his wife, Geraldine, live in Pittsburgh, Pennsylvania. They have four children—Joe, Bill, Rita, and Tom.

"Being born under the sign of the orange disc undoubtedly had some influence on my career," Jerry McAfee says with a grin. He is referring to the fact that he was born and raised in Port Arthur, Texas, where his father worked for forty years as a research chemist for Gulf Oil. At the time, the Gulf facility in the coastal Texas town was the largest refinery in the world.

The heavy-set silver-haired executive explains that he grew up in the oil business. "My first job was rolling barrels behind the Gulf experimental laboratory during the summer after I graduated from high school," he reminisces. "My task was to move several hundred barrels of oil from one location to another, and then to fill in with broken brickbats, and then to move the oil back again. That's what I did, all summer. In subsequent summers, I came back at progressively more technical jobs while I went to college."

Jerry adds that there's no better way to make a person appreciate what it takes to get a job done than to have the actual experience. "When you've worked your share of graveyard shifts," he says, "it helps you understand what goes on out there."

Jerry speaks evenly, with a slight Texas accent. "One of

my strong beliefs is that whoever sits in the chief executive's job should know at least one part of the business exceedingly well, on a hands-on, actual-experience basis. Whether it's marketing, refining, exploration, production, finance—whatever—he should know one of the major functions from stem to gudgeon. It would be ideal if he could know all parts of the business; but in one lifetime you can't do that. But it's very important, I think, that he know one part of the business extremely well."

Jerry himself had the opportunity to learn the chemical part of the oil industry exceedingly well during his early years with Gulf. Having obtained his doctorate in chemical engineering from M.I.T., he began with Gulf in 1945 in Port Arthur. He moved through various technical positions, and in 1954 was appointed vice president and associate director of research at Gulf's Research and Development Center in Harmarville, Pennsylvania. It was at this point in his career that Jerry began thinking about the possibilities of expanding into general management. He notes that to prepare him for the position, Gulf sent him to the University of Pittsburgh for an advanced management course, "Management Problems for Executives."

"I think some specialists object to the idea of moving into general management," he says, "and others who don't object should have objected. We've all seen darn good scientists turn out to be mediocre management people. I think it's important that there be concurrence between the individual and the company." In 1962, when Jerry moved on to head the Planning and Economics Department at Gulf's world headquarters in Pittsburgh, it was his first assignment in a non-technical area outside the refining field. In 1964, he was named a senior vice president, and relocated in London, where he had the broad responsibility for all Gulf operations in Europe, Africa, and the Middle East. He later moved to Toronto and eventually became president of Gulf Oil Canada Limited. In 1976, he was named chairman of the board of Gulf Oil Corporation.

During Jerry's forty years in the oil business, the McAfee

family moved twelve times. A devoted husband and father, Jerry admits that "moving is always tough on the family. It's really harder on them than on the executive, because he's put into a familiar environment. He has ready-made friends, associates—and a job to do." Looking back, Jerry says that the family's toughest move was from Port Arthur to the Pittsburgh area in 1950. "It was our first big move after we had our family, and we were leaving the area we'd thought we'd spend the rest of our lives in. We would be living in the big, bad north with the damn Yankees—up where it was cold and dark, and we didn't know anybody. I'll never forget what happened two days after we moved. Our oldest son, who was nine then, came up to me and said, 'Daddy, I've got twenty dollars saved up in my bank account. And I'll give it *all* to you if you take us back to Texas.' Now, that was a little hard on the heart."

Obviously, Jerry understands the mixed feelings some executives experience with such moves. "But I've been very fortunate to have a good relationship with my family," he says, "and there's always been the understanding that where Dad's job is, that's where we live. As a matter of fact, we came to realize that each relocation was a step forward. I have to believe that we all came out the better for it, because we had opportunities to make new friends, see new parts of the world, and share new experiences. When I think about those dozen moves, those opportunities have to be put down on the plus side."

Like other CEOs, Jerry works hard. He usually arrives at his office just before nine in the morning, and leaves around six-thirty. He doesn't always work at home in the evening, but he always takes work home. "I just like to have it," he says with a smile, "against the possibility that there might be a sudden snowstorm and I'd get snowed in with nothing to do." When he has to work weekends, he does, but by and large tries to resist the temptation. "However," he adds, "it would be misleading, and my wife would correct me, if I said I don't sometimes work on weekends."

Jerry believes that any businessperson must strive to achieve a balance between his work and his family. "If you don't realize this balance," he says, "you're neglecting an important part of life." A family-oriented man, Jerry speaks warmly of the role of his wife, Geraldine, in his own career. "A supportive spouse is about as indispensable as anything I know of," he affirms. "I certainly wouldn't want to try to live through my career without Geraldine's support."

Jerry's colleagues know him as an individualist with tremendous self-discipline. He has a reputation for running tight business meetings, opening with a comprehensive statement, keeping the discussion on the subject at hand, and deftly summarizing key points. He often expresses impatience to finish the job at hand and move on. In dealing with complex problems, he likes to separate the broad concepts from the detail and commit only the concepts to memory. For a CEO, he states, "a great deal of discipline is necessary. It would be entirely possible to fritter away all of your time on trivia. That's one of the big temptations of this job. There's so much trivia that it takes some conscious effort to say, 'Now, look, this is something somebody else can handle a lot better than I can.' So, as much fun as I would have doing it, I let somebody else handle it. Then I can spend my time on something somebody else can't do as well."

With the energy problems that have occurred since the 1973 oil embargo, Jerry has certainly not had any time to fritter away since he assumed the position of CEO of Gulf Oil. With assets in excess of $18.6 billion, and gross operating revenues of $28.8 billion for the 1980 fiscal year, Gulf is the seventh largest industrial company in the country. In 1980, the company had a net income of $1.4 billion, a return of 15.3 percent on average shareholders' equity.

With a tenfold increase in the price of oil during the 1970s, there has been much concern in the public sector that the oil companies have profited unduly. For a variety of reasons, the industry's growth in the share of total corporate profits has been significant. Many Americans believe that the oil industry is getting more than its share of total profits, and the public has been generally supportive of the windfall profits tax enacted on March 1, 1980, which was designed to prevent the oil companies from realizing excessive earnings.

Jerry applauds the government's program to decontrol the price of domestic crude oil, but he views the windfall profits tax as a hindrance to long-range energy development. The tax, he emphasizes, will divert during this decade an estimated $227 billion of vitally needed capital which could otherwise be used to develop American energy sources. He emphasizes that with the windfall profits tax added to existing taxes and royalties, the government will take about 85 percent of the incremental revenues generated by the oil companies. "Now, that leaves fifteen cents on the dollar for industry to plow back into finding additional oil and gas, digging new wells, building refineries, and developing alternate energy sources. Sure, fifteen cents is better than nothing. And, as a result, we're doing somewhat better than we have in recent years. But the fact is that most of the additional money consumers are paying for their energy today is not going back into the ground, as it were, but into the government treasuries. And only a very minor part of that revenue is earmarked for anything having any remote relation whatsoever to energy development. Some of it will undoubtedly go for welfare payments and other things which may very well be highly desirable *per se,* but those things have nothing to do with our energy problem.

"As for the question of oil company profits, it's important what you relate them to," Jerry says, gesturing with his glasses for emphasis. "It's practically meaningless to relate them to a prior quarter or year—that only indicates a trend. And it's just about meaningless to discuss them as a percentage of total corporate profits. Again, this is affected by many factors that have nothing to do with the matter. What is important is to relate oil company profits to the investment required to produce those profits. On that basis, the oil industry profitability is in the mainstream of all U.S. manufacturing. While it may be slightly higher at present, it's been considerably below average in recent years. It's just evening itself out right now.

"But I think what's of paramount importance is relating oil industry profits to the job the industry is expected to do. We have been held back for so many years in our efforts to develop adequate energy supplies for this country that we're now playing catch-up. This means we have to have even higher profitability than we have at present. Our capital requirements are simply enormous."

Jerry points out that Gulf, like other oil companies, has a tremendous need for capital to develop new energy sources. With 1980 earnings of $1.4 billion, Gulf invested nearly $3 billion in 1980—the first stage in an $18 billion five-year program. "In order to mount our program," he explains, "we will be dipping into the cash box considerably, and bringing our cash levels down. We will be disposing of non-productive assets, and may have to go into the capital market to borrow funds. But these are short-term measures. In the final analysis, the capital that we need to invest must be generated in the business. There's no other long-term source for it. We've got to generate the capital to do the job."

Energy projects inherently involve long lead times, and the oil industry is highly capital intensive. A company spends huge amounts on the hope of profits in the distant future. Jerry cites Gulf's explorations of Baltimore Canyon off the New Jersey coast as an example. "We were spending something like $70,000 a day," he says, "and it cost us $58 million without a discovery. Our original projection was that development would cost us a half-billion dollars—and if we were lucky, we'd get gas and oil ashore in ten years! Now, that's if everything had gone according to Hoyle. The Baltimore Canyon is just one example. But with any exploration, if there really are commercial quantities of oil and gas and we get lucky on the first strike and everything works out smooth as silk, it could still be ten years before we realize any revenue."

Gulf's North Sea program is another illustration. "In 1965, when I was coordinating Gulf projects in Europe, Africa, and the Middle East, we drilled our first exploratory well in the North Sea," Jerry notes. "We've only recently started to realize any revenue there, and it will be another three years or so before we get back what we have invested in exploration and development efforts—if everything goes according to plan.

"America *needs* big business," Jerry declares, shaking his head. "We are dependent upon giant corporations. If you look at Gulf's long-term expenditures, you can see that we have to have big corporations to do these things. Our exploration projects involve risk and time; it takes a great deal of staying power to wait them out."

Jerry believes that, ironically, one reason the public is so angry at the oil industry is that the industry did such a good job for so long. "After all," he points out, "until 1973 nobody gave a thought to energy except people who were in the business. Why should they? There was no problem. There was plenty of oil and gas and coal at a very, very cheap price. People thought it would always be like that. It took the oil embargo of 1973, and those long lines at the gas stations, to show the public that we had a problem—and cheap gasoline might not always be available. People were horrified. We'd always done such a good job that the embargo was an incredible contrast. I think that if we had not kept prices down, the public would be less shocked today and would react more favorably toward us."

Jerry's personal belief is that today's energy problem has its roots in 1954, when the Supreme Court gave the Federal Power Commission (as it was then called) the power to control the wellhead price of natural gas, which was at that time a distressed product. The FPC proceeded to control the price on the basis of what it had historically cost to find and produce natural gas as a waste by-product. "In retrospect," Jerry says, "this was a colossal mistake. Because, for a quarter of a century, it artificially depressed the price not only of natural gas but of all competing forms of energy as well—oil, coal, nuclear, and solar. As a result, we artificially encouraged the overuse of energy and discouraged its production. And people had no reason to think we had a potential problem. In my opinion, that's why it took us so long to even start formulating a sensible energy policy. We've made a beginning—but only a beginning. The one good thing the Carter administration did was to take the first steps toward decontrol of domestic crude oil prices."

Jerry believes the oil industry may face some of the same difficulties encountered by the steel industry. "The steel industry is having difficulty, because a generation or so ago the companies allowed themselves to be talked out of making legitimate price increases, increases that were absolutely necessary to generate capital for plant modernization. That's exactly the fate people in the oil industry are struggling to prevent. It could happen to us; the elements are there. We have the same need for additional capital. And the same pressures prevail. We simply must find a way to overcome those pressures."

Jerry's thoughts return to the problem of anti–big business sentiment. "It would be so foolish," he says, "if this nation would follow those groups who attack big business. Unfortunately, many people do. They want to stop America from using its big muscles. They want to tie our hands before the battle. It's utterly incomprehensible. Why shouldn't we use all the strength we can muster? In the energy industry alone, the task before us is so enormous that it's all we can do with our combined strengths—and even that may not be enough. But to think in terms of just using the little finger when we need the whole fist—it's unthinkable!"

The topic of the relationship between business and society is perennially popular with today's business leaders. Jerry believes that without question the corporation and society have responsibilities to each other. "Under our political system, the creative interaction between the marketplace and our social institutions is the fountain of our material wealth, and a foundation of our freedom. And the relationship between business and society may well be more complex today than ever before."

Jerry believes that the current uneasy relationship between business and society is the result of a historical phenomenon, an American renaissance. This social, political, and cultural revival began manifesting itself conspicuously in the early 1960s. Certainly it was rooted in many previously existing factors. Explanations for why it ballooned just then range from the youthful charisma of John Kennedy to the boredom of affluent "baby boom" students who felt a need for greater meaning in life. "Most of us who grew up in the Great Depression did not have that problem," Jerry states dryly. He enumerates the dramatic events the country experienced as the '60s wore on: "civil rights; the Kennedy assassinations, with the traumatic impact of shattered hopes; President Johnson's 'Great Society'; the rumored 'death of God'; Viet Nam; and—possibly the crowning catastrophe—Watergate, a shocking misuse of power at the highest political level."

Yet Jerry does not see the results of this renaissance as being entirely negative. "Yes, there was a resurgence of distrust in large impersonal institutions," he says. "But we have also seen a reaffirmation of the dignity and worth of the individual and his or her right to equal opportunity; and a fresh appreciation of the importance of our surroundings. In spite of all we hear about this country going to hell in a handbasket, the values reflected in this new American renaissance appear to me suspiciously old-fashioned—and are, in fact, part and parcel of the very principles upon which this country was founded.

"I believe that many of the social transformations we have witnessed—such as the ecology movement, the consumer movement, the women's movement, and the senior citizens' movement—are a rededication to our rediscovered principles. In spite of their occasional excesses, these social manifestations help improve society. I feel that business should face these movements. They're not just the figment of some malcontent's imagination. We must be sensitive to these changes and adjust to them, because they represent the new world that we're living in."

Jerry feels that a corporation's responsibilities to society boil down to three simple but important functions: to do the job; to do it at a profit; and to do it in accordance with the limits society imposes—ethical limits, environmental limits, and social limits.

In turn, he stresses, society has certain responsibilities to business in terms of those limits. Rules must be clear and consistent. They must be technically and economically feasible. Society must be prepared to pay the cost of these rules, not only of their implementation by business, but of their administration by government. They must be prospective, not retroactive. And finally, he says, let the rules set goals but not procedures. In other words, "Tell us what to do, not how to do it.

"By the same token," he continues, "government must understand more fully that part of its responsibility lies in making sure the messages we get are properly sorted out. At the moment, one agency issues a set of regulations saying, 'Do this,' and another agency says, 'Do that,' and it's left up to us to sort it all out. And that just shouldn't be our responsibility."

A case in point is the difficult issue of business practices in foreign countries—an issue faced by every large international company. "When companies do business in foreign countries," Jerry explains, leaning back in his chair, "they have to observe the customs, as well as the laws, of that country—or they're not going to be competitive. In other words, they're not going to be able to do business. Sometimes it is very difficult for a company or an individual to sort out just what the right thing is. At Gulf, our guideline is that we abide by the law of the land, and we conduct ourselves in such a manner that we would be proud to have all the facts known. Our policy is simple: to scrupulously adhere to the laws of the country we're in. And it's something we insist on without exception, as a condition of continued employment at Gulf.

"The difficulty is that in the real world it is sometimes hard to understand what the laws and customs of a country are. We say, 'When in Rome, do as the Romans do.' But it is not always clear just what the laws are. And when there are conflicts between the laws of another country and this nation's laws, it seems to me that that's a matter for the respective governments to sort out. It should not be left up to the private individual or corporation to make that determination."

Although he speaks with vigor and conviction, Jerry McAfee always remains calm. He pauses and glances out his thirty-first-floor window, which offers a distant view of the point where the Allegheny and Monongahela rivers meet to form the Ohio. The office itself is tasteful and rather small, considering the importance of its occupant, with an adjacent sitting room for meetings. The quiet informality reflects the man, who has been described as a person who "makes you feel comfortable—very much at ease." A popular personality throughout the oil industry, Jerry is known as a warm man who never resorts to intimidation.

Turning to the related problem of government regulation, Jerry thoughtfully quotes Thomas Jefferson: " 'Were we directed from Washington when to sow and when to reap, we should soon want for bread.' The energy industry," he continues, "perhaps even more than others, is being strangled with red tape. Take the windfall profits tax as an example. The number of lawyers, accountants, and auditors that will be needed merely to calculate it is staggering. The calculations have to be done on a property-by-property basis. Gulf has some 3,500 such properties. In addition, there are nineteen different price and tax tiers that can apply to any one oil field—and they are subject to change each month. Just computing the tax will involve a tremendous effort on the part of many people. And the possibility of future lawsuits arising from reinterpretations of the complex regulations is mind-boggling.

"Another example is the delay most new energy projects face. For instance, it now appears that it will require some eighty permits to get a synthetic fuel plant started. Many of these permits are sequential and have time limits. So if we don't get permit C in the required time, we could lose permits A and B and have to start all over again.

"In essence, we are being told 'when to sow and when to reap.' We are being told in such a detailed manner that the

American Petroleum Institute estimates that oil companies employ the equivalent of ten thousand full-time people just to comply with the regulations of the Department of Energy. This effort costs about $500 million a year—enough to drill over three thousand new on-shore wells. We simply must find a way to simplify the regulations."

Jerry points out that another major problem the energy industry faces is the government's withholding of public lands for energy exploration and development. He is convinced that, with due regard for environmental concerns, these lands must be made available on a timely basis. "A lot of people don't realize that about 30 percent of the area of this country is still in federal hands. Now, this 30 percent of America contains some of the most prospective areas from the standpoint of oil, gas, and other energy minerals. It has been estimated that it may contain half of the undiscovered oil and gas in our country. Yet, only one-third of this land has been made available to industry for exploration and production. The situation is even worse off-shore, where there are enormous prospects for additional oil and gas production. Believe it or not, in spite of all the work that's been done, less than 5 percent of our off-shore areas have been explored—much less made available for production. And the situation is not getting better, it's getting worse. There is a growing tendency for the government to withdraw more acreage from exploration rather than making more of it available."

Jerry again gestures with his glasses. "The tragedy of our present situation is that industry and government seem to be working against each other. But certainly the objectives of both government and industry are the same—to supply America's energy needs in the best possible way at the cheapest possible price. We ought to be working together to achieve these objectives, instead of being at each other's throats, as so often happens.

"Now, I have to temper this statement by adding that in some cases there is excellent cooperation between our company and others, and the government. A good example is our SRC-

II Demonstration Plant to be built near Morgantown, West Virginia. It will use the Solvent Refined Coal process that we developed to efficiently convert coal to a clean-burning liquid. It will be a $1.4 billion plant, the largest synthetic fuels project ever undertaken in this country. We've had excellent cooperation with the Department of Energy. Without that cooperation, there's no way we could justify putting that kind of money into the project. With air-quality requirements and social requirements being government controlled, government regulations will ultimately determine the economics of the project."

A consortium of Japanese companies headed by Mitsui and Co. and West German companies headed by Ruhrkohle AG is also involved in the SRC-II project. Jerry explains that the governments of Germany and Japan are participating as well. Gulf will be the operator and manager of the project and, as Jerry says, "the principal spark plug." The plant will ultimately be capable of converting six thousand tons of coal per day into the equivalent of twenty-thousand barrels of low-sulphur, clean-burning, primarily liquid fuel oil. From an environmental standard, this fuel will be more acceptable than the raw coal. Moreover, present studies at today's world crude oil prices indicate that the SRC-II fuel may become competitive with imported crude oil.

While synfuels such as Solvent Refined Coal may be important in the future, Jerry points out that they are not a quick solution to our energy problem. Commercial-scale SRC plants producing the energy equivalent of 100,000 barrels of oil per day are probably at least ten to fifteen years in the future. And coal and shale conversion processes demand incredible amounts of capital—more than twice the initial investment needed to produce the same amount of conventional oil. Beyond these hurdles, there are formidable legal, regulatory, social, and environmental obstacles to clear.

Like any CEO of a major corporation, Jerry spends a major portion of his time in long-range planning. "If a chief executive doesn't realize that part of his job is to provide for the long-term health of the company, as well as the short-term, then he doesn't have a very sound appreciation of the job he's in. It's got to be a fundamental principle that the long-term concern is part of the job; it isn't appropriate to look only to short-term profits. That doesn't mean you neglect the short-term, however. Again, the CEO's task is to try and strike a proper balance."

As Jerry nears retirement, he is frequently asked what he plans to do when he is no longer CEO of Gulf. He shakes his head and smiles. "I've got a full-time job here, just trying to fight the battle of this job. So I haven't given the future after Gulf much thought." As those close to him will attest, Jerry's personal future is a less urgent concern to him right now than his search for the long-term solutions to America's energy needs.

One of Jerry's prime concerns is this country's failure to fully develop its conventional energy sources—oil, natural gas, coal, and nuclear power—which he believes to be our only significant choices for at least the next decade. This failure, he points out, places the United States in an increasingly vulnerable strategic position. "In 1979, this country imported more than 8 million barrels of oil a day," he stresses. "According to economists, when you consider the projected rate of growth in our consumption of energy, our imports could increase to 10 million barrels a day by 1990. That is a doleful state of affairs.

"Moreover, some two-thirds of all the oil that moves by sea in international trade comes from just five countries, which all border the Persian Gulf. Anything that stopped the flow of that oil would immediately plunge the economies of the industrialized world into chaos. About half our imported oil comes from that troubled area. The oil-producing countries in the Middle East control the world's crude oil spigot, and many of them have made it clear that they would not hesitate to turn it on—or off—to meet their own economic or political ends."

Jerry is quick to point out an optimistic side, however. "The

United States has an abundance of resources that can be developed," he emphasizes. "It's estimated that there is as much gas and oil waiting to be found as has already been produced. Our known high-grade shale reserves are almost as great as the oil reserves of Saudi Arabia. Our coal reserves (which can be converted to synfuels) are estimated to be thirty times greater than our proven crude oil reserves. We have substantial uranium resources, plus solar, biomass, and nuclear fusion, which can make a contribution in the more distant future."

As one of this country's leading authorities on the subject, Jerry believes that the United States does not have an energy shortage in the absolute sense of the term. Instead, he says, economic, environmental, legal, and bureaucratic restrictions are making it impossible for the oil industry to extract our natural resources. It is his belief that four actions must be taken immediately in order to make it possible for the United States to realize its energy potential. He notes that all four areas for action are equally significant, and that all have many ramifications.

"First," he asserts, "it's essential to permit the development of sufficient capital in the energy industry so that we can do our job. This means adequate profitability, and the freedom to retain an appropriate proportion of our revenues. To underline this need for capital formation, let me mention that, as agreed at the Tokyo Conference, the United States is to hold our oil imports to the 1978 level of 8.5 million barrels per day for the next decade. That means approximately 6.2 billion barrels of domestic crude oil and natural gas equivalents must be found every year—or one and a half times what the industry has been able to find in recent years. To do this, the best estimates are that the industry's capital expenditures for conventional oil and gas exploration and production must double—in constant dollars—by 1990.

"Second, to realize our energy potential, it is absolutely necessary that the government make more federal land accessible for oil and gas exploration and production—both on-shore and off-shore land. I just cannot overstate the importance of this issue. In effect, we as a nation are tying our own hands. We're saying we have an energy problem, and yet we're not willing to develop the potentials we've got.

"Third," he says, shaking his head, "somehow we've got to clear out the regulatory quagmire. Not only the oil industry but all American industry is operating under every kind of environmental and social restriction today. I agree that most of them have a good justification in themselves. But in many, many cases, they have simply gone too far. I think it's not so much a matter of doing the wrong thing, but of doing the right thing to excess. Often there is no regard for the costs involved. We need to get on the basis of examining the *cost* of these requirements. Once we do that, we can put the cost up alongside the benefits we expect to derive from the regulation and ask ourselves whether we as a nation are prepared to pay that cost.

"The fourth action is at least as important as the other three, and that is the need for more cooperation between industry and government. The lack of that cooperation is one of the tragedies we face today. We've got to learn to work together instead of against each other. Now, a certain degree of 'creative tension' is healthy, but it's gotten out of hand. We need to devise better ways for government and industry to work together. Look at the tasks we face: loosening the grip of OPEC on our economy; finding and producing our hydrocarbon reserves; developing the advanced technologies for synthetic fuels. These jobs are just too big, and the risks are too great, for either industry or government to even try to handle them alone.

"I keep repeating," he concludes, "that the petroleum industry's most important message to government is simply this: 'Tell us what you want done, but don't tell us how to do it. Tell us the destination, but don't tell us how to get there. Leave the doing of the job to the ingenuity of the industry!'"

Jerry's concern for America's energy needs extends beyond his role as CEO of Gulf. Perhaps his statement at a recent annual shareholders' meeting best summarizes his ideal:

If we are successful, it doesn't just mean that Gulf will be a bigger and stronger and more profitable company. It means that the nation will have more energy resources, will be less dependent on foreign oil imports, and will enjoy a stronger economy. It also means that you will share in these rewards—both as a shareholder and as a citizen. That's what we're working for . . . that's our goal.

7

David W. Mitchell

CHAIRMAN OF THE BOARD AND CHIEF EXECUTIVE OFFICER,
AVON PRODUCTS, INC.

Dave Mitchell joined Avon in 1947, at the company's Pasadena, California, manufacturing laboratory, where he was initially employed as a mailboy. He served in various capacities in Pasadena until 1960, when he was named branch operations manager of the company's Sales and Distribution Branch in Morton Grove, Illinois. He later served at Avon's New York City world headquarters as director of sales training and as national city sales manager. He was elected vice president of sales promotion in 1964, group vice president in 1965, senior group vice president in 1967, and executive vice president in 1968. In 1971, he was elected to the board of directors, and in January 1972 he became president of Avon. He was elected chief executive officer of Avon Products, Inc., in January 1976. On March 3, 1977, he assumed the additional post of chairman of the Board of Directors.

Presently Dave is a member of the board of the New York Life Insurance Company, American Machine and Foundry, Inc., and the Dry Dock Savings Bank. He also serves on the board of the National Minority Purchasing Council, Inc.

He is a member of the board of the Fountain House, the

Economic Club, the National Golf Links of America in South-ampton, New York, the Clove Valley Rod and Gun Club, and the Links Club, New York.

Born in Pasadena, California, on January 14, 1928, Dave has one daughter, Marcia Zeller, and a seven-year-old granddaughter, Morgan.

Today the Avon product line, which was launched by David McConnell in 1886 with five fragrances, includes over seven hundred individual items. If all the shades of makeup and different fragrances and styles of fashion jewelry are included, the total more than doubles. The extensive line includes something for everybody: makeup, skin-care, fragrance, and bath products for women; cologne, talcum, and after-shave for men; grooming products for children and teenagers; and collectible decanters and jewelry for every member of the family. Through Avon Fashions, the company also sells wearing apparel by mail. In the beauty business, fashion and taste change rapidly, and so does the Avon line, to keep pace with—and set—the trends. Avon typically introduces more new products in a single two-week campaign than many cosmetic companies do in a year.

As chief executive officer of Avon, David Mitchell heads the world's largest manufacturer and distributor of cosmetics, fragrances, and costume jewelry. More than 1.2 million representatives sell Avon products in the United States and twenty-nine foreign markets, making it by far the largest sales organization in the world. The New York–based company had $2.57 billion in consolidated net sales in 1980. In a multibillion-dollar industry, Avon Products, Inc., is the undisputed world leader.

At age fifty-two, Dave Mitchell is relaxed and confident as he discusses his career with Avon. Of course, he should be at ease in the company—Dave joined Avon at nineteen, and has been there ever since. So the blond, boyish CEO has earned the right to feel at home in his spacious thirty-sixth-floor office overlooking Central Park.

"After I graduated from high school," Dave says, "I had enrolled in the University of California at Davis, with the intention of becoming a veterinarian. But when I realized how many years it would take, it didn't look so good. Finally I decided to head back to Southern California, where I worked a couple of interim jobs; but I was still looking for the right thing.

"My stepfather, who was a pharmacist, had a cosmetic line called Marie Arnold," Dave recalls. "He and his mother owned the business. He compounded and mixed the cosmetics in a very small store, just scratching out a modest living, so that I helped with family expenses as a matter of course. When I got the Avon offer, I had two other job offers pending, and Avon was the lowest paying. But I took the position on my stepfather's advice. He told me, and I'll never forget how he said it, that the cosmetics industry was 'going to grow like the blazes.' He knew that I could start off making more money somewhere else, but he believed this was the business to get into. Actually, I was just looking for a job with pleasant people, and I liked the people I'd talked to at Avon. That probably had as much to do with my decision as any other factor. I have to confess that at nineteen I wasn't thinking too far into the future. I certainly wasn't thinking about someday being an executive. I was more interested in the present—I wanted a steady job!

"So I went to work for Avon in Pasadena, in what they called—and still do—the Service Department." He grins. "In other words, the mailroom. My starting salary was $140 a month, and my job included anything a clerk-mailboy might do: sorting mail, taking distribution around through the offices,

DAVID W. MITCHELL

running errands, operating a manual Addressograph machine, all the stuff you do when you're low man on the totem pole."

In his sixth month in the mailroom, the company ran an ad in a local paper for a production control clerk. The applicants were instructed to write to a post office box, and Dave's job was to pick up the letters, open them, sort them, and deliver them to Personnel. "I couldn't help but read the letters," he admits, "and I began to see that those guys applying didn't have any more background for the position than I did. Actually, I thought I might be more qualified. At least I knew something about the company. So I got up the courage to approach Personnel and say, 'Look, I'd sure like a shot at that job.' Well, they evidently couldn't find anyone else, because they gave it to me."

As a production control clerk, Dave watched inventories and estimated sales. "I'd have to figure out the batch sizes for manufacturing," he explains, "how many pieces would come from five thousand pounds of cream, and that sort of thing." He also began to learn more and more about the company. At this point in Dave's career, Avon seemed very large to him. Yet, over the next thirty years, he was to watch its United States manufacturing facilities double, from two plants to four, while additional facilities went up abroad. The 25,000 representatives selling Avon products when he joined would total nearly 1 million by the time he became chairman. The sales volume, increasing 35, 40, or 50 percent some years, would climb from $17 million in 1947 to well over $2 *billion* by 1980.

Gradually Dave moved closer to the heart of this enterprise, growing with it. Shortly after he became production control clerk, he was given his second promotion, this time to production supervisor. "It was the first time I directly supervised anyone. I don't mind telling you I was somewhat apprehensive. I literally walked out onto the production floor the first day to see 115 people looking to me for direction. Well, I was young and energetic, and I worked hard and learned the job, and from the first I loved it. They were great people to work with, those women who processed and packaged the products. And it was a fast-moving job that required a sharp eye for sales trends and that sort of thing. After a while, even though I was just in my early twenties, I started to think that maybe I had a chance to advance in management. I had learned that I really enjoyed working with people, and the people seemed to like me, too. I'd had no idea that I had that kind of ability; it was a revelation to me. And I began thinking about the future."

From his position as production supervisor, Dave was especially struck by the possibilities in sales. "We had two division sales managers in the Pasadena branch," he recalls, "and it was clear that they were the guys who were making money. They drove the big cars, and wore the expensive clothes. In addition, I knew they got bonuses at the end of the year if sales were up, and we were growing by leaps and bounds. But there I was, getting basic salary and no bonus.

"You have to remember that I had firsthand experience in being poor. Even to this day, I think that experience, deep down inside, continues to drive me. I had worked from the time I was fourteen, handling a paper route and working at an A&P, and my money had been needed. It bought my clothes and went toward the rent. When you come from that kind of experience, financial security is important. I knew what it was to worry where the money would come from if someone in the family got seriously ill. So the economic advantages of being in sales were very appealing to me."

When a division manager's position became available, Dave applied for the job, only to be rejected because of his age; he was twenty-five at the time. "They hired a fellow from the outside," he says, "and of course I was disappointed. But as it turned out, he only lasted six months. And when the job opened up a second time, I got it.

"It was a terrific job, very challenging. My basic responsibility was to hire, train, and motivate a staff of district managers, all women. I had working for me between fifty and sixty women, who in turn would appoint the representatives. My territory covered the major cities on the West Coast, Alaska, and Hawaii, so the job required a lot of travel. In those days, our trips often lasted two or three weeks. Today, a division manager will fly out and be back in a couple of days. But the travel was sweetened by the fact that Avon always believed in doing things right. We flew first class, and we stayed at the best hotels. There was a lot of responsibility, but a lot of excitement, too. Some years our sales would double!"

As a division manager, Dave trained the district managers to locate and appoint sales representatives. "We were expected to do our share of field work," he recalls, "and I did. If a manager couldn't find a representative in a given territory, she would take one side of the street and I'd take the other, and we'd ring doorbells, asking people if they could recommend somebody who might want to be an Avon representative." Dave did his share of door-to-door selling, too, testing new sales kits and brochures, and refining presentations. "You can imagine the reception I got from women expecting an 'Avon Lady,' " he says, smiling.

In 1960, Dave made the first of his two moves for the company when he transferred to the Sales and Distribution Branch in Morton Grove, Illinois. Although his new position as branch operations manager was an internal position, with responsibility for shipping, accounting, billing, inventory, and so on, his appointment was still sales-oriented, since his primary function was to service the representatives. "It has always made sense to Avon," he explains, "that the person in charge of servicing representatives should have selling experience, so he or she can relate to what's going on in the field." Once again, Dave worked long hours and learned the job quickly. As he recalls, he had just mastered it when he was moved again, this time to Avon's world headquarters in New York City, where he became director of sales training.

From that point on, Dave Mitchell's career was meteoric. He was appointed national city sales manager, and in 1964 elected to vice president of sales promotion. A year later he became a group vice president, and two years later, in 1967, senior group vice president. In 1968, he became executive vice president, in line for the presidency of the company. Three years later, he was made a board member, and in 1972 he was elected president of Avon and chief executive officer. The ascent had been amazingly swift. With a wide grin, Dave agrees. "You know, there was one fellow who used to like to grumble, 'The reason Mitchell moved along so fast was that he never held a position long enough to fail at it!' "

Dave is quick to say that one reason for his rise is timing. "I was very fortunate to arrive at the New York headquarters when I did. It was during a period when the company was just growing very fast, and that kind of expansion opens up opportunities. Also, there was quite an age gap between the older executives, who had been with Avon from the early days and had their eyes on retirement, and the younger group. The older executives wanted to groom the younger fellows for management, so it was a very good time for me to be there."

Today, Dave's relaxed manner and informality suggest the total confidence that often marks the men who lead enormous corporations. This kind of confidence grows through years of learning new jobs, doing them well, and receiving promotions. But Dave stresses that he was not always so sure of himself. "In fact," he confesses, "every time I took over a new position, I had my doubts as to whether I was really ready to handle it. I'd think, 'Maybe there are things about this job that I don't know about, things I have to do.' I'm sure a lot of people react this way to new responsibility. But I had a habit of throwing myself into it, and before very long I'd be able to step back and see that I really did know how to do the job."

Certainly one of the chief reasons Dave's career with Avon has been so spectacular is his simple old-fashioned willingness to work. From his early days to the present, he has had the habit of coming in at seven-thirty in the morning and staying until about six. He also takes work home for review in the evening. "I guess I always have worked a little harder than some of the other people around me. Maybe it was really insecurity—maybe I felt I had to put in extra effort to keep up. But I always had the idea that you just did the job, whatever it took. I remember, when I was in the manufacturing end, standing out on a railroad spur at nine at night waiting for a freight car. And then I helped unload it, so the bottles and labels were ready and production could start at eight the next morning. Of course, I loved what I was doing. That's what made it possible to work so hard.

"I've often wondered," he continues, "why I kept putting in these hours. Sure, it was understandable during those early years. But now, I guess it's just a matter of habit." Could Dave's position be handled in an ordinary workday? "Sure," he says, "but you'd have to delegate a lot more than I do, so you'd lose some control." He shrugs. "Maybe that would be a good thing. I really don't know. It just doesn't happen to be my style, that's all."

Dave freely admits that throughout his career his work with Avon has had top priority in his life. "It's hard for me to imagine someone doing *this* job," he says, tapping his desk, "who didn't feel that way. It may sound self-serving, but the truth is, Avon has been my whole life, from the time I was nineteen until today. My job has always come first. And I think it takes that kind of total commitment to get maximum results. We have fifty-three officers at Avon, and it's easy to pick out the people who are dedicated to what they're doing. They're in here early every morning, and they're still here late at night. They're people who perform. If you tell one of them about an out-of-town problem, he'll say, 'I'll go out there and take care of it,' and he's out there as soon as possible. Then there's another few people who come in at nine and leave at five, and I'm not saying they don't do a good job, because they do. But they don't have the same dedication to their work. They lack that total commitment. And no question about it, it takes that extra effort.

"As I look back," he comments thoughtfully, "I do sometimes say, 'I wish I hadn't devoted so much time to my work.' There's no question about it, when you do, it's detrimental to your family life. It's one of the things I really don't like about myself. Still, it's probably not realistic to wish you'd done things differently. After all, here I am, still coming in at seven-thirty in the morning, exactly what I say I wish I hadn't done. I think that, like many executives, I feel guilty sometimes about not spending enough time with my family. We tend to rationalize, and say, 'Look, I'm working for you.' And we tell them, 'What I'm achieving here, the monetary gain, the retirement benefits, these things are really going to come to you.' Naturally, wives and children don't quite see it that way, and I'm sure they're right. Whether an executive wants to admit it or not, he's primarily working to fulfill his own ambition in life. He's only fooling himself if he thinks otherwise."

To hear Dave talk, you might think his association with Avon has been one long love affair. Although this is by and large true, there was a time when he nearly left the company. "Back in the fifties, when I was a division manager," he recalls, "there were some things happening that made me feel I was being treated unfairly. And then I got caught in a personality conflict between two of my superiors, which I shouldn't have been involved in in the first place. So I was pretty unhappy. I discussed it with my family, and they encouraged me to resign. I thought it over, and finally I went to my boss and told him I was leaving. Well, he asked me to delay my departure and attend a division managers' conference in Houston. I didn't want to go, because I expected to feel uncomfortable with the other managers. But, fortunately, I went. When I got there, I was invited to the suite used by top management.

"The men that talked to me there really gave me a shot in the arm. I learned that they thought more highly of me than I had realized. They also pointed out the opportunities for me with Avon, opportunities which, looking back, I suppose I had never really doubted. But it was hearing how they felt about me that really impressed me. It's very good to know your work is appreciated. As a result of that talk, I stayed, and that's the only time in thirty-three years with Avon I've even considered leaving."

In spite of his spectacular success, Dave has had his share of failures along the way. "Several years ago," he recounts, "when I was vice president of sales promotion, I became convinced that we could improve our service to our representatives by having them telephone in their orders for merchandise rather than mailing them. I put a lot of time and effort into developing this idea, because I believed we could realize a dramatic increase in the number of customers a representative could serve. Finally we tested it in Springdale, Ohio. When it didn't work at first, we changed it, and changed it again. We spent a lot of money, and tried everything, but it just wouldn't pan out. The cost payout was not feasible."

Dave also remembers a more recent mistake. "Back in 1975, we were trying to acquire Monarch Capital Corporation, our first real acquisition attempt. Well, the idea was poorly received on Wall Street, and the bankers and other 'experts' were very negative. Frankly, I couldn't take the heat. Finally I made a decision and said, 'Look, we've got to cancel this.' If I had not done that, we would own the company today—and it's done tremendously well. Monarch is a very well run company, and it's been successful. We should have stayed with it, but I let us get talked out of a good thing. I made the wrong decision, that's all."

Like every other executive, Dave has also had his share of people disappointments. "There are times when I have really counted on someone to grow and be available for a big job, but for varying reasons it didn't work out. That's always a disappointment. But I suppose it's bound to happen when you work with people."

By and large, however, Dave's experience with people at Avon has been good. The consensus there is that he has a remarkable ability to relate to employees who work under him. "He doesn't just supervise," one manager says, "he motivates people." "Dave leads by example," another notes, "and that is the most effective type of management there is."

"I like to maintain close contact with Avon personnel," Dave explains. "I think the secret of building good rapport is to *listen to what people have to say.* I always try to be a member of a group, rather than the guy who's obviously running the show. I've often said to other executives that if I'm out to dinner with several managers, I'd like to believe an outsider couldn't pick me out as the boss." Refusing any credit for this modest attitude, Dave explains, "I'm a shy sort of fellow, and I don't enjoy the limelight. If I can help the company have favorable publicity, I'll do it; but I avoid personal publicity. I kind of think that philosophy permeates the organization to some extent."

Feeling as he does, Dave refuses most requests for newspaper and magazine interviews. Although he is frequently offered awards by various civic groups wishing to hold dinners in his honor, he almost never chooses to accept. His modesty is apparent in other ways. Unlike many New York VIPs, he dislikes using a chauffeur-driven limousine, a perk that usually accompanies the position of CEO. "It makes me feel ostentatious," he says uneasily. "Only when I have to, will I use a driver, and then I tell them to send an unpretentious car, something ordinary."

This kind of down-to-earth behavior is unusual in the world of fashion and cosmetics. Equally unusual is the fact that Dave Mitchell gained his position without the benefit of a college education. A living example of an individual who has been educated on the job, Dave is proof that experience is still the best teacher of all. His management is outstanding, his knowledge of business principles thorough, and his expression of ideas clear and articulate. An avid reader, he studied books on management and marketing constantly for many years. In his early career, he also devoured such magazines as *Business Week, Fortune,* and *Forbes,* learning about business, he says, not as it is taught, but as it is done. But he claims that the best education he got was on the job: "I went out and observed Avon's approach to marketing, and then I did it myself. I experienced it day in and day out. Not only did I read the sales manuals but I ended up writing some of them, when there were marketing techniques I thought should be introduced." His ideas were always encouraged, he says. "Of course, at Avon we're good listeners. The company has always been receptive to new ideas. If something looks good, we'll test market it; and if it works, we'll incorporate it as standard procedure."

The youthful-looking CEO leans back in his chair. "In terms of education," he says slowly, "I think by far the biggest help for me was studying the people I worked for. There were several executives I tried to emulate because I respected their styles of management. Although I took various American Management Association courses, and learned something from each one, my real training was done on the job by those people above me."

When asked if any one person was especially influential, Dave replies, "Several, really. But if I had to single out just one, I'd have to say it was Wayne Hicklin, the chairman prior to the one I succeeded. Wayne has an exceptional mind for selling, and I learned a lot from him about marketing. But his biggest strength is his ability to work with people. He's incredible. He could fire you, and you'd say, 'Jeez, I really appreciate you firing me,' and walk out of his office loving him. He just had the knack of getting people on his side. I respected his ability to work so effectively, and I carefully observed his skills."

Although Dave has held positions at Avon in both administrative and marketing operations, and has enjoyed both areas, he prefers the marketing end of the business. He notes that most of Avon's top executives have marketing backgrounds. In fact, he says, in the past, marketing and field experience have almost been prerequisites for advancement to top positions. As one who began as "low man on the totem pole," Dave firmly believes that this approach is best. "This is a field you don't learn in a classroom," he emphasizes. "You can't go to Harvard or Stanford to find out how to run a direct selling company. Avon is unique, and not the kind of corporation that can be run by textbook techniques. Now, we do recruit our share of young people from the big schools, but we still put them through the ranks. There just isn't any question about it—in our business, the day-to-day roll-up-your-sleeves get-in-there-and-fight approach is essential."

Dave finds his past experience in lower ranks useful on a daily basis, and has no difficulty illustrating this fact. "If someone comes to me and says, 'Look, we've got a problem on the dock, and this is the way we've got to do it,' I can understand what the problem is. I may not have been down to the dock for a while, but I've worked on it, so at least I have a feel for when somebody might be giving me a snow job. And I know that's true also in other areas. Advertising, promotion, merchandising, shipping, branch operations—you name it, and I've had some association with it."

Like most large corporations, Avon now tends to recruit college graduates for many positions, especially in areas such as finance, where educational background is necessary. While Dave supports this policy, he never forgets that this was not always the case. "We hired a young college graduate recently," he says, "and sent him to Rye. He was a bright fellow, and I thought he'd do well. But the general manager called me when he got there and said he wouldn't do. 'We're looking for men with experience,' he complained. I said, 'Wait a minute. If that policy had been in effect when you and I applied, we would never have been hired!' Well, he had to laugh and agree that *that* would have been a calamity!" Dave insists that not only can an inexperienced person learn and progress at Avon, but that a high school graduate like himself could come in today and be where he is thirty years from now. "With hard work and strong motivation," he says, "that could still happen. The door to the executive suite is always open for good people. I really believe that, and I hope I'm right. Give me a person with commitment, and I'll show you top executive positions available for him or her."

Responsibility at the top of Avon is traditionally shared by a triumvirate, Dave explains. Dave, as chairman, Bill Chaney, Avon's president, and Jim Preston, the executive vice president, are on the board of directors. There is an established line of succession. When the chairman retires, the president usually becomes chairman, and the executive vice president moves to the presidency. During Dave's presidency, when the chairman suffered an illness but wished to remain as head of the board, Dave was also named CEO.

Surprisingly, when he reached fifty-two this year, Dave Mitchell qualified for full retirement. While retirement age at Avon is the standard sixty-five, the company also uses a rule of eighty-five: an employee whose age and years of service total eighty-five may retire with full pension. Dave does not intend to retire yet, but doubts that he will stay in his position until he is sixty-five. He enjoys talking of those remarkable people who work into their eighties, and reminisces about Charles Tiffany, who ran Tiffany's (now a wholly owned Avon subsidiary) until past his ninetieth birthday. "But that's not for me. Maybe I feel this way because I was so young when I started with the company, but I just don't want to work forever. I'm in the camp of people who favor earlier retirement. But it's a personal choice, and I don't condemn anyone who feels differently."

When he does retire, Dave plans to move to his 160-acre farm in Connecticut, where he can be found almost every weekend. About two hours from his Manhattan apartment, the farm is another world for Dave. "I play at being a farmer," he says with a grin, "pitching hay, driving the tractor. I love it. When I retire, I'll plant trees and raise cows. It may never be an economic success, but that's not the point. It's just great fun, and very relaxing. Of course, like any place, it's the people who really make it. Up there, it's a very different way of life, and I've made some good friends, like a seventy-six-year-old farmer who lives near me. In the winter, when there's not so much to do, I go over to his place or he comes to mine, and we sit in the kitchen by the stove, and enjoy a drink. I just love that. We trade ideas, and believe me, those people's views of the world are not what you'd hear in Manhattan."

Dave admits that there are those who don't think he can give up his commitment to hard work and enjoy that kind of life, but he disagrees. "I don't intend to be a hermit, after all," he says. "I'll probably travel south in the winter, and then there are a few trips I'd like to take with my grand-daughter, Morgan. So I won't be pitching hay all the time.

"But you know," he reflects, "being on a farm gives you plenty of time to think, and I value that. Sometimes when I'm on the farm I wonder what my life would have been like if I had become a veterinarian. Much more peaceful, I think. But what might have been doesn't bother me. I've enjoyed my career. If I had it to do all over again, I wouldn't change a thing."

THOMAS A. MURPHY

8

Thomas A. Murphy

CHAIRMAN OF THE BOARD AND CHIEF EXECUTIVE
OFFICER,
GENERAL MOTORS CORPORATION

After receiving a bachelor of science degree in accounting from the University of Illinois in 1938, Tom Murphy joined GM as a clerk on the comptroller's staff in Detroit. Fifteen days later he was transferred to the Financial Staff Offices in New York. There he held successive positions as accountant, statistician, and supervisor of corporate forecasts and financial analysis. In 1954, he was named director in charge of analysis of corporation and divisional pricing. Two years later he was directing the financial analysis section in the treasurer's office in New York.

In 1959, Tom was appointed an assistant treasurer. He moved to Detroit to become comptroller of GM in 1967, and treasurer in November 1968. In March of 1970, he was elected vice president and group executive in charge of the Car and Truck Group. On January 1, 1972, he was made vice chairman of the Board of Directors, and a member of the Finance and Executive Committees.

He was elected chairman of the Board of Directors and chief executive officer of General Motors Corporation on December 1, 1974. He is chairman of GM's Finance Committee and a member of the Executive and Administration committees. He is a member of nine GM policy-making groups:

Energy, Industrial Relations, Public Relations, Marketing, Personnel Administration and Development, Product, Research, Service, and Overseas.

Tom was the 1978–79 chairman of the Business Roundtable. In addition, he is a member of the Board of Directors of the United Negro College Fund; a director of the University of Illinois Foundation; a member of the Financial Executives Institute; and a member of the board of the United Way of America. He is also a director of the Overseas Development Council; a founding member of the Business and Professional Friends Committee of the National Center for State Courts; a member of the Executive and Financial Committee of the Business Council; and a management member of the Labor-Management Group. The American Legion has awarded him its Public Service Medal.

He has received honorary doctorates from Fordham University, Canisius College, Rosary Hill College, Tougaloo College, the University of Detroit, DePauw University, Iona College, New York University, College of Mount St. Vincent, Wayne State University, and Notre Dame.

Tom was born on December 10, 1915, in Hornell, New York. He entered the U.S. Navy in 1943 and was discharged in 1946 as a lieutenant (j.g.). He and his wife, Catherine, live in Bloomfield Hills and maintain an apartment in New York City. They have three children, Mrs. Catherine A. Rowan, Mrs. Maureen Fay, and Thomas A. Murphy, Jr.

As chairman of the board of General Motors, Thomas Murphy heads the largest manufacturing company in the world. GM produces 46 percent of all cars sold in the United States, including imports. Worldwide, the company accounts for 21 percent of all automotive sales. In 1980, with net sales of over $57 billion, GM employed almost 850,000 people. The leader in an industry which directly or indirectly employs one out of every six working people, GM is an important factor in American life.

The responsibility of serving as chairman for a company with assets in excess of many nations is awesome, but Tom Murphy views it matter-of-factly. "Many jobs look overwhelming to an outsider," he says, "and every job has its tough parts. If you let that overpower you, you'll never break the job down to its elements and get on with it. Any job that has been done before is essentially manageable; it has to be, or no one could really fill it."

Tom Murphy not only fills his job, he appears born to be the chairman of the board. Approaching retirement, he is still trim and energetic. A Hollywood producer would undoubtedly think he was perfect for the part. The gray hair suggests wisdom. The rugged face is reassuringly intelligent. The square jaw indicates toughness. Behind the horn-rimmed glasses, the eyes are perceptive and youthful. He emanates vitality. The part of chairman of General Motors is not easy to fit; Tom Murphy is obviously perfect.

It is natural to assume that an individual like this would have always known that ahead of him lay the chairmanship of what many consider to be the greatest corporation in history. Paradoxically, this is not so. In fact, Tom Murphy's working life began with hard labor, and his college education almost did not come about.

After graduating from high school in 1932, Tom got a job at a Cicero, Illinois, icehouse owned by City Products, for whom his father worked. "It was not a good time to graduate," he says. "It's hard for people who didn't live through it to understand what it was like back in the Depression. You had to be in it to feel the dimensions of the unemployment. Today we think 6 percent unemployment is bad, and of course it is. But back then it is estimated that unemployment reached 25 percent—and that represented almost entirely heads of households, so it had more impact than 25 percent unemployment would today."

Feeling lucky to have the job he did, Tom worked as the "vault man" at City Products, stacking the 400-pound cakes of ice on end. "It was exhausting work," he admits, "the kind of labor that makes your bones cry out at the end of the day. But it was a job, and during those days there just wasn't work to be found. So I did it until September, when I was laid off. In those days most people didn't have mechanical refrigeration, and they depended on ice. But when the fall came and the weather cooled off, business cooled off too, and there was no more work for the summer people."

Tom then joined the ranks of the unemployed. His search for work futile, he occupied part of his time that winter by taking courses in shorthand, typing, and bookkeeping at the local high school—hardly the preparation you would expect for a chairmanship. But Tom, at eighteen, was not thinking of chairmanships in the future; he just wanted a job.

The next summer he was rehired at the icehouse. Happy to have work, he still knew he would be laid off again in September. "There was a guy working there," he recalls, "who was attending the University of Illinois. We did that hard, cold work side by side, and finally one day he said to me, 'Are you going to be around here breaking your back for the rest of your life? You'd better get out and get some more education—or that's exactly what you'll be doing.' I don't know whether it was the icehouse or what he said, but I felt chilled. Because when I thought about it, I knew I didn't want to work as a vault man forever.

"So we would talk about it, and he would tell me again that I had to go to college. And I would say I couldn't afford it. But he argued that he did it by working summers at the icehouse, and I could do it too, with maybe some odd jobs during the school year."

If Tom had an ambition in life at that point, other than simply working, it was to be a professional baseball player. He grins. "That's what I really would have liked to do. But I just didn't have the inherent talent, and I could never have played up to the standard of the major leagues. If I could have, that's what I would have done, though; the glamour of professional baseball was very appealing."

The year since Tom graduated from high school had been discouraging. Yet, he maintains, he was lucky that things went as they did for him. "I was out at Stanford University a few years ago, and the kids asked me, 'How do you get to be the chief muckamuck in a big corporation?' I guess the simple, straightforward answer is luck. I told them, 'I had a great advantage. I graduated from high school in 1932, and a few months later I was unemployed. I recognized that getting a job was important—that it was something you had to get, and after you got it you had to work to keep it.' "

Tom's parents encouraged his desire to go to college, and finally he decided he would. "But I had no idea what to study," he says. "I just hadn't thought about it. That autumn my mother drove me down to the University of Illinois to register, and she waited with me in line. When I got to the front of the line, I would have to declare what college I would enter, so she asked me what I was going to choose. Up until that time, I hadn't thought about it. I liked athletics, and the fellow at the icehouse was a phys ed major, so it entered my mind that I could do that. But I considered it for a minute there, and decided I wasn't quite that interested in sports. So I said to my mother, 'I don't know as I'd want to be a coach.' About that time I was at the head of the line, and I remembered the bookkeeping courses I'd taken at the high school. So when the fellow up there asked me, 'What school do you want?' I said, 'Put me down for the College of Commerce.' And that was that."

Tom Murphy modestly credits much of his success to luck. It would seem to be lucky for him that he had time, standing in that line at the University of Illinois, to change his mind about his major and begin the business career that has taken him to the top. But the talent for leadership is hard to hide. It seems likely that if he had chosen phys ed for a major, Tom would not have ended up coaching at a high school level, but would have been destined to manage the Yankees or coach the Steelers.

In college, Tom's liking for sports led him to a football career that was, however, uneventful. Since he had played basketball for the local Elks Club, he was ineligible for football under Big Ten rules until his junior year. By then, immersed in studies, he had decided not to try out for the team. But he went down to school a week before classes started to help his younger brother enroll. "I had nothing to do," he explains, "so I checked out a football uniform and went over to the practice field. The team was scrimmaging, and I stood around with a few other guys watching them. Well, the coach was short a lineman for defense, so he pointed at me and told his assistant, 'Get the big guy.' I wasn't huge—six feet one and two hundred pounds—but I was the biggest guy there. So they put me in.

"They figured I should be a soft touch, being green, so they tried to run the first three plays over me. Now, I'm not mobile, but I was in good shape from working at the ice house, and I couldn't be budged. So I made the team."

Tom is quick to point out that he has never been a person with the uncanny ability to excel in all endeavors. Leadership, yes. He did become captain of the B team. In his own words, "In all candor, I have to say I was no great shakes. You have guys who can run forty yards in 4.4 seconds. I probably never did it faster than eight."

It is often said that all great endeavors begin with one small step. In the summer of 1937, Tom took a step that seemed small at the time; he went to work for General Motors in New York City. "They offered me a summer job," he recalls, "for about a hundred dollars a month. When you came down to it, that would just about pay my expenses, so I didn't think it was worthwhile. But my parents encouraged me to take it. They thought it would be a great experience for me, and they offered to take care of my college expenses the next year. So I worked in the company's financial offices, and then went back to school.

"When I graduated the next year, General Motors offered me a full-time job at the comptroller's office in Detroit. I was there for about fifteen days, and then they asked if I would mind going to New York to work in the financial offices there on a temporary basis. I agreed. What started as a temporary assignment lasted twenty-nine years!" When Tom Murphy, who started in Detroit as a clerk in the comptroller's office, came back to Detroit, it was to assume the post of comptroller.

As he settled into his job in New York, Tom didn't have the faintest idea that he would climb the corporate ladder to the top. "You have to realize," he says, "that when I started, it was a time when jobs were scarce. I just wanted a job, and I considered myself lucky to find one with a good company. Beyond that, I didn't think about it. I just applied myself to my work.

"I believe we all worked hard back then. After all, if an individual didn't perform, there were a dozen people ready to move right into his job. So it was up to you to perform well and show that you were worthy of the position. If you didn't, well, you didn't have a job!"

Did Tom ever think he might someday become chairman of the board of General Motors? "Never," he answers quickly. "Never in my wildest dreams."

By the time Tom was hired, GM had surpassed Ford to become the biggest automobile manufacturer in America, yet he never felt he was working for a huge, impersonal concern. In the New York offices, there were fewer than a hundred employees—hardly a monolithic organization. "My whole concept of General Motors was more or less on that scale," he says. "Many people have the idea that working for a big corporation makes you a tiny cog in the machine. But I don't think there's that much of a difference between working for a large company and working for a small one. Your relationships always tend to be in a rather small arena, with a relatively small number of people, whether the organization is local or multinational.

"You may work in a small store with a few people, meeting customers every day; or you may work for a huge chain. You're still working with the same people day to day. We're all part of a country which has a population of over 200 million. But we don't feel lost in the maze. Each of us lives with his own family, in his own home, in his own neighborhood. Each of us has neighbors and friends. In a sense, the big corporation is the same way."

Tom was in his fifth year at the New York offices when he was drafted. At the time (1943), the office had already lost staff to the armed services, and those who remained were working long hours six days a week. "We were all drained," he recollects, "physically and mentally. In fact, I was at the point where I was wondering if General Motors was the place for me. One weekend I had gone home almost ready to quit. There had been a reshuffling at the office, and I felt I'd been pushed aside. If the next day had been a working day, I might very well have walked in and said, 'If that's the way you feel about me, I'm going someplace else.' But I talked it over with my dad, and by Monday morning I had decided to show them that if they thought I didn't have the ability, they were mistaken.

"The military service came at the right time to give me perspective on all that. I entered the Navy as an enlisted man, and was commissioned and sent to Supply School. There I was thrown in with guys who came from backgrounds similar to mine, and who complained about their own career problems. It dawned on me that my situation wasn't peculiar to me, that in fact I was better off than a lot of them. Still, when I got out after the war, I looked at other opportunities before I decided that General Motors offered me the most opportunity. Once I had convinced myself of that, I never again considered leaving the company."

The years after the war went smoothly for Tom as he worked in various capacities in the New York offices. Then in October 1953, he developed a rare virus in the intestinal tract. "It was the biggest setback of my life," he says. "My job was demanding, but I loved it. Suddenly I was being told that I had to stay in the hospital for three months and rest at home for another three months. It seemed like the worst thing in the world that could have happened, and I have to admit to feeling sorry for myself.

"Fred Donner, who became chairman of General Motors, was the vice president in charge of finance at the time. Just as I was talking this over with the doctors, he called me. When he asked me, 'How are things going?' I guess I was still in shock. Anyway, I really let it all go when I answered him. Then he said to me, 'Tom, you're probably feeling pretty sorry for yourself right now, and understandably so. If you let yourself, you can make yourself very unhappy—and everyone else around you as well.' He told me to concentrate instead on the positive aspects: I had good health care, good medical benefits, a job waiting when I got well, a family that loved me.

"So I tried. Advice like that is easily given, but it's hard to accept, and I'm not sure I appreciated the wisdom of what he said. But I made myself try to put things in perspective. I'd say to myself, 'Look, what's the big deal? In twenty-five or thirty years, this won't seem so important.' And, as I look back on it now, I can say that's true. It wasn't such a big disaster after all.

"Still, I had to fight self-pity. One day as Christmas approached, I was very bored lying in bed in Roosevelt Hospital, and I still felt depressed. Then the door to my room flew open and my wife, Sis, and our kids came charging in. They jumped on the bed, hugged me, and showered me with gifts. Suddenly I realized what a lucky guy I really was, because that illness gave me time to rediscover my family. I had been working long hours and making frequent business trips, and perhaps I had neglected to recognize my children as individuals. But that illness, and especially the three months at home, brought us together."

He smiles broadly. "I've been very lucky. I married a woman who did a great job with the family. She felt the home and children were her job and the office was my job. I managed my part of it, and it was up to her to manage her part. When there was a minor crisis, Sis would handle it and only tell me about it afterwards. I'd get home to find out a kid had dislocated a knee, or banged a head, or the furnace had quit, or someone had dented the car. I'd say, 'Why didn't you call me?' And she'd always look a little surprised. It never occurred to her to call me. She just handled it."

It is sometimes said that the corporate world demands too much personal sacrifice of the ambitious executive. Tom doesn't feel that to be true. "I think you'll find success-oriented people in all walks of life driving themselves at a similar pace," he declares. "Successful professional people, small entrepreneurs, people with deadlines to meet, they all sometimes reach the point where they have to put everything else aside and say, 'Okay, here's what I have to do.' Whether it's a big corporation making the demands, or the individual putting pressure on himself, those of us who want to do a good job sometimes have to blot out everything but the work at hand and do it."

Tom has worked long hours during his career at GM. How long? "I don't know if I ever bothered to count," he replies. "I've always worked about the same hours I do now. I'm at the office at eight in the morning, and I get out of here about six-thirty." Pressed, he admits that he usually takes a couple of briefcases home with him on the evenings when he is not traveling or speaking somewhere. Some people claim his two briefcases keep him in shape. "They're so heavy, it takes a major man to lift them," says a friend, "and Tom Murphy is a major man."

In view of his demanding schedule, Tom makes an effort to keep in good condition. "I used to walk to work in New York," he says, "so I probably got more exercise then. Here I can't walk to work. But four years ago, my wife bought me an Exercycle, and I've built that into my daily routine now. I get up half an hour earlier than I otherwise would, and work out on that, do some pushups, that kind of thing."

However, Tom credits his energy and capacity for work to his ancestors. "Obviously, some people have more physical stamina than others. In my judgment, it's simply a matter of having picked the right genes. The Lord gave me a good constitution, I'm thankful to say.

"I have another God-given gift," he says with a smile. "When I go to bed I usually fall asleep without much tossing and turning, and I rest well. People who can't do that are really at a disadvantage. Nobody's forces are bottomless. You have to restore yourself. You can handle problems much more successfully if you can rest. I only sleep about six hours a night, but it's good sleep."

Although his responsibilities as chairman of GM are heavy, Tom is able to walk away and relax. In fact, he claims that he is under less pressure now than during his early years with the company. "In those days, the economic pressures were severe. 'Am I going to have a job?' 'Will I be able to keep it?' 'Will I make enough money for the vital necessities?' I think the individual at that level has more pressure than the one at my level. Not that I don't think about my work when I'm away from it. But the pressures are of a different type, a different dimension."

Tom emphasizes the necessity of keeping perspective in a job like his. "I know that by myself I can accomplish some things," he says. "But it's going to take a lot more than Tom Murphy and his office to get this company doing the things that are necessary to serve customers. I devote my time and energies on a day-by-day, hour-by-hour basis to the things I can address, and I try to make sure the other people in General Motors understand their individual responsibilities. It's essential to have people you can rely on, and then to go ahead and rely on them."

Although Tom came up through the financial end of the business, he stresses the human side of management. "Good communications, understanding, and strong personal relationships—these are the most important aspects of operating a business," he maintains. "Of course, you address the problems and try to come up with imaginative plans and programs. But you've got to realize that the best plans won't work unless people understand what they are supposed to do and how they contribute to the overall plan. If they understand and support the plan, it will work. But the best plan will fail if they don't."

Executives who move up into the stratosphere of a large corporation often have progressively less contact with workers on different levels. "In my position as chief executive officer," Tom comments, "I have to reach out and keep myself tuned in to what's happening in the company. I need feedback to make decisions, and I have to rely on the people who report to me to get that input."

He smiles. "I've often said that I miss the rumor mill. When I was down in the bottom of the organization, I could keep in on the grapevine. In fact, I could put a few rumors of my own into circulation. That's the fun of life at times. As chairman of the board, I don't hear any good rumors. I'm kind of insulated. They don't tell me where the rumblings and grumblings are. Of course, I still have a few cronies I pump once in a while."

Yet, Tom is not as close as he'd like to be to many of the people he has worked with during his career. "I'm afraid there's a tendency to feel a little less comfortable with somebody who has donned the mantle of high office," he says. "Some people feel they can't be quite as candid. And while most people deny it, I believe in all honesty there's bound to be some resentment. Someone is bound to think, Boy, he was a numbskull and I knew it. He was just lucky to get beyond me. I've got more ability, but somebody didn't like the way I part my hair! "

Tom is aware that people may also think that politics plays a part in the rise to top executive status. "If it took the craft of a politician," he says, "I don't think I'd be sitting here." He gestures at his office and clasps his hands. "If I have a view on a subject, I'm the kind of person who makes it known. And I might not be diplomatic, particularly if I feel strongly about it. I have to admit my bias, but I do believe there is very little politicking here. There's no place for it. There's a place for diplomacy, sure, so people can get along agreeably, and try to get their ideas across without alienating others. But ingratiate yourself with others to advance your career? I don't think that works in this atmosphere."

From the first, Tom was absorbed in his work rather than in the possibility of advancement. As a result, he has more than once been surprised by promotions. One of the biggest surprises came in 1967. "I had started on the comptroller's staff in 1938," he explains, "but I spent my entire career on the treasurer's staff in New York. In 1967, it was announced that the company's comptroller was retiring. Being in the New York offices, I felt I was out of the mainstream, and I never considered myself a candidate. Besides, there were half a dozen good candidates on the comptroller's staff, and several others in the rest of the financial organization.

"I was on vacation in Florida, and the vice president in charge of finance called me. He said, 'I just want to bring you up to date and tell you who the new comptroller is going to be.' I thought, That's nice of him. Then he said, 'It's you, if you'll take the job.' " Tom did, and later that year the family moved to Detroit.

Tom's appointment to the office of treasurer a year later was equally surprising. "It was more by accident than design," he explains. "Frank LaRowe, who had been my boss when I was assistant treasurer, was the company treasurer. He became ill and had to retire suddenly. Before I knew it, I was treasurer."

At that point, Tom thought his career at GM had reached its peak, since all his experience was in the financial end of the business. "Then one day," he says, "I was summoned to the office of our chairman, Jim Roche. Other members of the Executive Committee were there, and Mr. Roche began telling me about some changes they would be making in the company organization. Well, we'd all been hearing rumors, and I thought, Great. Since I'm an officer, they're going to tell me what's going on before I read it in the newspapers.

"He went through the whole thing, and at the end he said that Pete Estes, who had been in charge of the Car and Truck Group, was going to take over the Overseas Division. He continued, 'And we had in mind that you would be taking his job.' My first reaction was 'You gotta be kidding!' So I said, 'Mr. Roche, I have a lot of respect for your judgment, but I'm a bookkeeper. I was born and raised in finance. I can count on my fingers the number of GM plants I've visited.' But they wanted me. He was very complimentary about the work I'd done in other capacities, and he told me they were sure I could do the job. So I took it, and then I ended up here."

Here is the chairman's cluttered office. The consensus at GM is that the man who occupies it today is as down-to-earth as ever. The desk is littered with files and reports. To prevent misinterpretation, a sign proclaims, "A cluttered desk is a mark of genius." Another sign reads, "Please don't

straighten up the mess on my desk—you'll goof up my system."
Being a Murphy, Tom is of course a believer in Murphy's
Law: "If anything can go wrong, it will go wrong, and it
will go wrong at the worst possible time." But his own law
for General Motors appears on another sign on his desk. He
interprets the sign, sent by the GM subsidiary in Germany,
as Murphy's Second Law, one he established for GM: "If everybody does his job completely, nothing can go wrong."

Despite the clutter, Tom manages to be organized. His system is his own, but it works. "They say if a person handles
the same piece of paper more than once, he's not a good executive," Tom remarks. "By that standard, I'm not a very good
executive, I guess. Instead of having my secretaries sort my
mail, I have it placed in my box and I sort it myself. Of
course, they've developed their own system, and they put material they know I should look at on top of the heap. They
place requests for my time on top, and underscore any deadlines
that have to be met. Then I make a quick cut through all
this and make decisions. Many things I'll look at two or three
times. Some things I'll take and say, 'Okay, this is something
I have to spend some time thinking about,' and I start the
thinking process then and there. Other things get put aside,
but that doesn't necessarily mean I'm through with them."

Tom's attention to detail is legendary at GM. Executives
joke that he is the best proofreader in the place, since it is
not unusual for a report or memo sent to him to be returned
with a punctuation mark or typographical error corrected.
He admits that he does this mechanically. "I like to kid that
I read the last page first and make sure to find a misspelling—
just to convince people that I read the whole thing."

However heavy his workload, Tom approaches meetings prepared, and insists that others do the same. He believes in circu-
lating an agenda so everyone knows in advance what will be
discussed, as well as distributing relevant material to those
who will be attending. "If people come prepared," he asserts,
"a meeting can move and be productive. A good executive
should be ready to think about the subject, talk about it, and

move toward a decision. That's just conducting business in a businesslike fashion."

As chairman, Tom must have some working knowledge of many areas of the business unrelated to his financial background. He stresses that he relies heavily on experts in other fields, such as manufacturing and engineering. "The one thing I have learned is the jargon," he says. "You have to know what they're talking about. And I've learned enough of the technical end to keep up with the technicians in a conversation. That doesn't mean I have to know how to design an automobile. It isn't necessary to know everything. What is necessary is to know your own limitations, and make sure you get people who compensate for them.

"Of course, there's still a tremendous amount to learn," he admits, "and I learn by reading and by talking to the people with the knowledge. It's really up to me to reach out and try to understand. My position is no different in that way from that of any other executive. Every individual must constantly learn about his business. If he doesn't, he's retrogressing."

Tom emphasizes that an individual from any area in GM can become the chief executive officer. "I don't think any one background is better than another," he says. "While my predecessor, Dick Gerstenberg, was primarily a financial man like myself, others have had backgrounds in engineering, manufacturing, marketing, and other areas. Every executive starts out with a specialty, and at some point in his career he has the chance to make the transition from specialist to generalist." Tom illustrates these roles with the story of two men. "They're both doing the same thing," he says, "cutting rocks. When the first man is asked what he is doing, he says, 'I'm cutting stone.' The second man, however, replies, 'I'm building a cathedral.'

"The generalist," he continues, "has to be like that second man, able to look at the broad context. While some people are competent in their specialties, they may not be willing to make that transition. A financial man may want to remain in the financial end of it. An engineer may want to remain in engineering. They simply don't want to be involved in general management."

Tom explains that GM continually reviews and evaluates people's capability and performance, with an eye to determining who the people are who will run the company in the future. Because of unforeseen health problems as well as mortality, a company such as GM has to develop considerable depth in its management team. For this reason, the company attempts to give its executives the background and experience to handle various top management roles.

He adds that this system is reassuring. "It's comforting to be chairman and know there are capable people in the wings who could lead this corporation, literally dozens of them, with the talent and willingness to do a good job. In the past, I've seen some very capable men occupy this office, and it was hard for me to conceive of General Motors turning a wheel without them. But the company has always continued to grow as one chairman stepped down and another took his place. And I know when I'm gone, the company will run without me. That's not modesty. That's a fact, and a fact I'm glad for."

Upon reaching the mandatory retirement age of sixty-five, Thomas Murphy will end his forty-third year of service at General Motors. Under the company by-laws, he can continue as a board member for five years after his retirement, "if," he says, "they will have me." As chairman, he is the only individual in active management who is permitted to continue as a board member after retirement.

It is notoriously difficult for busy executives to face retirement, but Tom is already confronting that problem with the optimism so typical of him. "It will be a good opportunity for me to do things I haven't been able to do," he muses. "Perhaps serve my family a little better. Not have to respond to the alarm clock every morning. I don't look at retirement as the world saying, 'We're finished with you, and the parade has passed you by.' I look at it as the chance to do things you've wanted to do. And"—he grins—"*not* to do things you don't like."

Tom Murphy will be remembered as one of this country's great business leaders. As he steered GM through the energy crisis of the 1970s, he proved an articulate spokesman for the entire automobile industry. Under his leadership, GM's capital expenditures have been greater than ever in its history, as the company invested billions of dollars in meeting tighter emission and safety standards. In downsizing the traditionally bulky GM automobile to a more functional vehicle, the company took a big gamble and won.

General Motors has made great strides during Tom's six years as CEO. Today, 23 percent of the cars produced throughout the world are GM products. Tom's competitive ardor shows when he talks about this fact. "If we're selling 23 percent," he exclaims, "that means our competition around the world is making and selling three cars to our one. Imagine the opportunities that exist for us at the international level!"

Tom does not hesitate to say that he hopes GM will one day get the lion's share of the automotive market, both in this country and abroad. Presently, 47 percent of all cars sold in the United States, including imports, are produced by GM. "You can be sure we'll be competing for *every* car sold in this country to be a General Motors product," he declares. He is, of course, aware that there are those who frown on this kind of ambition. "They equate bigness with badness," he says, "which betrays a very cynical suspicion of success. Many companies in many industries are big, but none were born big. Their size is the consequence of their success. And even if there are only a few large competitors in an industry, that doesn't lessen the competition. You wouldn't say that the finals of an Olympic race are less competitive than the Boston Marathon, even though the Boston Marathon has many more contestants.

"Of course I want to win every one. It's like a football coach. He may tell his team at the beginning of the season, 'Look, we're scheduled for fourteen games, but I'll be satisfied if we win half of them.' Nevertheless, he's going to go out and try to win every single one, because the games are played one at a time. It's the same way with selling a product. You're not going to get every single customer, but you have to aspire to. You have to go out there with a positive approach and convince everyone in the organization that, by gosh, the goal *is* to sell them all."

The distinguished-looking executive taps his desk for emphasis. "Our *job,*" he says, "is to do the best we can to sell every customer—by offering the best value. That means making a superior product and following up the sale with superior service. We believe in obeying the laws of this country, and I think one of the unwritten laws behind our economy is that you have to be strongly competitive. That's right! If we obey all the laws, including that one, and we compete by doing the best job, the end result will be that customers will favor GM by giving us their business. And whatever percentage of the business we get—if we earn it—it's ours. It's our reward for doing the best job."

Consumer choice, Tom believes, is the best assurance of quality production and a strong economy. "There are some people," he asserts, "in and out of government, who would substitute regulation by government for consumer choice. They aim to assure that competing firms achieve equal results. When you stand back and look at it, it's hard to believe, but lawsuits have actually been filed based on the theory that it is unfair for a company to offer better values or lower prices than its competitors." Tom believes overregulation is a real danger not only to American industry but to the individual consumer. "In too many cases," he says, *"government regulation is taking the form of government direction.* This, I believe, leads to the loss of individual choice."

To illustrate his point, Tom cites the case of a small businessman named Joe Pinga who operated a bakery in Rhode Island. Cited by OSHA (Occupational Safety and Health Administration), Pinga refused to pay ninety dollars in fines. Instead he spent $1,500 fighting the citations in the courts. To Tom,

Pinga's citations seem to typify the worst of overregulation—a safety railing four inches too low; electric plugs with two prongs instead of three. Pinga, a second-generation American, was quoted in *Time* magazine as pointing to a thick volume of OSHA regulations and saying, "If this book had existed when my dad came to this country in 1907, this country would still be a prairie. Now it's bureaucracy on top of bureaucracy. That's not America."

Tom frowns. "That kind of thing is happening time and time again. Somehow we've got to get a better relationship between what we gain from these regulations that are forced upon us and what it costs us as a society. I most certainly am not against safety in our factories. I'm all for it. But when the regulators get into the act, they tend to make a complicated mess out of an otherwise simple thing, and common sense flies out the window. Suppose there has to be a guard rail on a stairway. They can wrangle endlessly on the question of how high it should be. You might say about three feet. Okay, do you mean thirty-six inches is the only acceptable height? Can somebody get a citation for a thirty-seven-inch rail? When it's all said and done, regulations end up creating far more expense than is necessary. I know the idea is that OSHA is making the workplace safer. That means they automatically assume that it's unsafe to begin with. But if you examine the statistics, you'll see that the average workplace is safer than the average home!"

Tom leans back in his chair. "You know, I understand their good intentions. I suppose all of us from time to time think we could do a better job than the people in government are doing; but I really think the great majority of them are talented and dedicated to improving the system. It certainly isn't perfect, and I'm a big believer in working toward making it better. But it can go too far. Unfortunately, too many government people think that the average American really isn't able to look after himself; so the government, they think, has to make choices for the people."

Tom is very concerned about maintaining American freedom

of choice. "The greater the role we assign to government," he says, "the smaller the role we assign to ourselves—and the more inhibited our freedoms become. If we have learned anything from recent history, it should be that government is very good at some things and very, very bad at others. The government should confine its activities to its areas of competence. Even the liberal Senator Gary Hart from Colorado has said, and I quote, 'As a result of Watergate, as a result of Vietnam, as a result of budget deficits and the failure of a number of public and governmental programs, people are questioning . . . whether government, in fact, can solve all the problems.' "

These, Tom believes, are questions of vital importance to America's future. He quotes Senator Hart again: " 'We're at a historic crossroads in our economic system. We either preserve our free-market system, or succumb to a quasi-socialistic economy.' We often hear it said that it can't happen in the United States of America," he continues, "but the sorry example of modern Britain stands before all of us. There are many who fear that America is only a generation away from the fate that is befalling Great Britain. There you have a country that tried to live in never-never land, where the government would solve every problem and all citizens should share equally. And it isn't working. Even a former Prime Minister, a member of the Labor Party, said, 'We will fail if we think we can buy ourselves out of our present difficulties . . . by paying ourselves more than we earn.'

"We have to learn a lesson from England and teach it to those Americans who are urging our country to seek the same degree of social welfare and income redistribution that has brought that great nation to its present troubled state, where the shares are becoming more equal—but progressively smaller."

Tom firmly believes that there is not another economic system in the world that Americans could emulate in whole or in part that would not cause our quality of life and our standard of living to go down. "On purely humanitarian grounds," he insists, "free enterprise proves superior to any other system, for the simple reason that its greater productive efficiency produces more wealth for distribution—not by arbitrary sharing, but by providing the incentive to increase the pie for all."

Much of General Motors' success under Tom can be credited to his integrity and genuine desire to benefit others through his work. He believes that while every business has an interest in profits, no enterprise can succeed for long unless it makes a significant contribution to the society of which it is a part. He emphasizes that this is not his attitude alone, but one which pervades GM: "From the day I started as a clerk in the comptroller's office to the present, I can say with all conviction that I have never been asked to do, and never done, anything I would be ashamed of. There has never been anything I could not proudly explain to my family. I have not had to compromise my personal standards to get a job done—it is not necessary. And I would like to think everyone at General Motors can say the same."

Long years of difficult decisions and great responsibility have done nothing to lessen Tom Murphy's vitality and enthusiasm for life. "Some people," he remarks thoughtfully, "take a negative attitude from the day they're born. They seem to say, 'Forget it all. I'm going to die, and that's the reality.' That thought governs their existence. Perhaps it leads them to give up trying, or even to take their own lives. But I don't think the human spirit is quite that way. I think we instinctively battle for survival, fight to make our own lives a little better."

A man of great humility, Tom does not claim sole credit for his success. Instead he says, "When I look at the great opportunities I've had just because I was born in America, and born to good parents, I find it easy to respond positively to challenge. I've had so much. And when I think of the sacrifices our ancestors made settling this land, and I consider what they endowed us with, I am overwhelmed with the desire to contribute to the well-being of this great country."

9

James D. Robinson III

CHAIRMAN OF THE BOARD AND CHIEF EXECUTIVE
OFFICER,
AMERICAN EXPRESS COMPANY

Jim Robinson began his business career in 1961 with Morgan Guaranty Trust Company, where he served as an officer in various departments. In 1967, he became an assistant vice president and staff assistant to the chairman and the president of Morgan Guaranty Trust. The following year he joined White, Weld & Company and was named a general partner in the Corporate Finance Department. In 1970, he joined American Express as an executive vice president. From 1971 to 1973, he additionally served as president and chief executive officer of American Express International Banking Corporation. In 1973, he became the group executive vice president responsible for Travel Related Services, as well as chairman of American Express Credit Corporation. In 1975, he was elected president of American Express Company.

In April 1977, he was elected chairman and chief executive officer of American Express Company. He also serves as a director of American Express Company, American Express International Banking Corporation, Fireman's Fund Insurance Company, and various other subsidiaries of American Express.

Jim was born in Atlanta, Georgia, on November 19, 1935.

He graduated from Georgia Institute of Technology in 1957. From 1957 to 1959, he served as an officer in the U.S. Naval Supply Corps. He received his MBA from Harvard Graduate School of Business Administration in 1961.

In addition to his directorships with American Express, Jim is a director of Bristol-Meyers Company, the Coca-Cola Company, Trust Company of Georgia, and the Union Pacific Corporation. He is a member of the Board of Overseers and Board of Managers of Memorial Sloan-Kettering Cancer Center and vice chairman of Memorial Hospital for Cancer and Allied Diseases. He is also a member of the Business Council and the Business Roundtable; the Advisory Council on Japan-U.S. Economic Relations; the Board of Trustees of the Brookings Institution; the Council on Foreign Relations; the Economic Club of New York; and the New York Stock Exchange Listed Company Advisory Committee.

Jim's other affiliations include the Rockefeller University Council; the Pilgrims of the United States; the Board of Directors of the New York Chamber of Commerce and Industry; and the Economic Development Council of New York City, Inc. He is on the Board of Governors of United Way of America. He was the 1980–81 chairman of the New York State Savings Bond Committee.

Jim and his wife live in Manhattan. They have two children, a daughter and a son.

"Do you know me?" Most people identify American Express with this phrase and the high profile of its credit cards around the world. The company began in the express industry; it was founded in the 1840s by a man named Henry Wells, who transported gold, silver, financial papers, and securities from Albany to Buffalo. In 1850, Wells teamed up with his major competitors, and a new entity called American Express Company was formed.

During the Civil War, American Express made its services available to the U.S. government for transporting vital supplies to Army depots. Election ballots were delivered to the troops in the field, and parcels were delivered to their families in the newly overrun Confederate territories.

It was after the Civil War in 1891 that the company invented and began issuing its now world-famous traveler's checks. Today, American Express has extended its range of services to include insurance, international banking, communications, and entertainment. In 1980, the company had assets of approximately $20 billion. Revenues were $5.5 billion, with a net income of $376 million.

This diversified giant is headed by Jim Robinson, who was elected its chairman and CEO in 1977, at age forty-two. Jim

Bachrach

JAMES D. ROBINSON III

is one of the youngest individuals ever to head a worldwide financial institution.

Born and raised in Atlanta, Jim comes from a family of bankers; his father was chairman of the First National Bank of Atlanta, as was his grandfather. When asked how he happened to break a Robinson tradition, the dynamic executive says, with a still-noticeable Southern accent, "I guess I'm the black sheep in the family—the only one who went north."

Looking back to his youth, Jim says, "I was a long time zeroing in on what I wanted to do. Banking was one possibility. I'd worked one summer at First National Bank—but then I'd also worked as a laborer at a brick company." At Georgia Institute of Technology, Jim majored in industrial management, making Dean's List and graduating in 1957. He then entered the Navy Supply School for six months, and spent the remainder of his two-year stint in the service as a disbursing officer for the submarine base at Pearl Harbor. "I suppose I began to get more serious during my time in the Navy," he says. "I joined the Toastmasters, and I took the New York Stock Exchange correspondence courses. That's when I actually made up my mind that I wanted a career in finance."

After getting out of the Navy, Jim worked briefly in Atlanta as a security analyst for the Trust Company of Georgia, and then entered Harvard Business School. It was an enlightening experience for him. "I went up there thinking that perhaps I had a head start, because I'd been a security analyst and taken the correspondence course," he says with a sheepish grin. "It only took me about three days to realize that some of my associates, particularly those who had gone to Eastern schools, were a lot smarter than I was. They might be English or history majors and not know business, but they had learned to think. The competition was really tough. I had to run the 440 while they were running the 220—just to keep up."

After receiving his MBA, Jim entered Morgan Guaranty Trust Company's training program in 1961. "I spent my first few weeks," he says, smiling, "pushing those little black carts with securities up and down Broad Street." Jim went through several departments, and ended up five months later in the money market area. Two years later, he moved into the newly established Merger and Acquisition Department. From there he went into the commercial banking area and then into the Investment Department. (Coincidentally, while in the bank's Commercial Banking Division, Jim was the junior officer on the American Express account.)

In 1966, Morgan Guaranty offered Jim "a fantastic opportunity"—which he nearly turned down. "Tom Gates was the chairman," Jim explains, "a wonderful person. He had been Secretary of the Navy and also Secretary of Defense. Tom was looking for someone young to act as aide and assistant to him, having worked with that kind of setup in the Navy and Defense.

"One of the executive vice presidents told me Tom wanted me for the job. My first reaction was 'Gee, I've never had so much fun as I'm having in the investment area. I'm doing exotic financings, and I'm working with a fantastically bright group of people. I'm not so sure I want to give that up.' But, of course, I said I wanted some time to think about it.

"So I called my father for his advice. I said, 'Just wanted you to know that I'm going to turn down being the chairman's assistant.'

"He replied, 'Wait a minute! You'd better sit down and have a martini and think about that one some more. It's a marvelous opportunity to see how an organization works from the top down.'

"My father and I were very close, and I had tremendous respect for his opinion. So I sat down and had that martini and thought about the offer some more. And I realized that I really hadn't considered it as broadly as I might have. So I took the job. And working with Tom Gates turned out to be a tremendous exposure to some fine people, to a sense of values, and to Morgan's professional way of doing business."

In 1968, intrigued by the investment banking business, Jim joined White, Weld & Company as a partner in the Corporate Finance Department. Two years later, Eugene R. Black, former head of the World Bank and a longtime friend and adviser who had helped Jim think through some important decisions in the past, approached him about another opportunity. He raised the question as to whether Jim would be interested in a senior position at American Express.

"I vividly recall telling him," Jim says, " 'Gene, any time you suggest something, it's worth thinking about.' And six months later I came on board here as an executive vice president. I expected to be involved in the financial area. However, the company was going through some reorganizational studies, and a month after I joined, they asked me to become president of their American Express International Banking Corporation. They wanted me to help build the management strength and develop that part of the business."

Jim grins and shakes his head. "At the time I was thirty-five, and I'd only been outside the United States once in my life. All of a sudden, I was responsible for an organization that ranged from Copenhagen to Bangladesh. Quite an experience."

In the summer of 1972, Jim hired Dick Bliss, who replaced him in March of 1973, when Jim moved over to the travel-related Services Group. Still serving as executive vice president, he was now the executive responsible for the group that includes the Card, the Traveler's check, and the Travel divisions.

At this point in his career, Jim was ahead of schedule. He had developed the habit, since his graduation from college, of setting short-term career goals. "It was a step-by-step process," he reveals. "I knew I needed to add this, and I'd have to add that along the way. I was willing to bet on myself— to bet that I could learn. I thought that if I delivered, my track record would speak for itself. I'm a great believer in having a game plan, and in setting your targets high. Obviously, a person who does that, and is willing to make the personal commitment, can achieve a great deal more than one who is less demanding of himself.

"When I was at Morgan Guaranty, I set a kind of series of matrices in terms of where I wanted to be at age thirty-five, at forty, at forty-five, and so on. I looked at it as a five-year, ten-year, and fifteen-year program. I knew I needed certain experiences to achieve those goals. Actually, it was just a way of collecting my thoughts. To date, I guess I've been ahead of schedule.

"As I said, I believe in setting my targets high," Jim says. "When I came here, I knew that Howard Clark, who was CEO at the time, wanted the option of retiring at age sixty. There were no promises, but that was his game plan, and I was one of the candidates for the position. So I came here with a clear objective—if not the CEO, then one of the top positions in the company." He smiles. "If you don't swing at 'em, you don't hit 'em."

In 1975, with Howard Clark's recommendation, Jim was named president of American Express. "We had a lot of fun working together," Jim says of his predecessor. "We had different styles in some ways, but we shared similar viewpoints on objectives. He was a good friend. I learned a great deal from him, and I have tremendous respect for him." In 1977, Clark, who led the company so successfully for seventeen years, stepped aside, and Jim was named chairman and CEO of American Express. When asked about Clark's recommendation of such a young man for the position, Jim jokes, "I think he figured he could get me to spend more time on this or that, or change certain methods, or even improve my golf swing—but the one thing neither of us could do anything about was my age. So he accepted it."

The CEOs of large institutions have typically spent most or all of their working lives in those companies. Jim had risen to the top position at American Express in only seven years. Such a transition would probably not have been possible for an individual who came into the company from an unrelated field. But Jim's financial experiences at Morgan Guaranty and at White, Weld gave him a useful background from which to step into a position at American Express. "Our product is financial and insurance services," he points out, "so the transition was possible. It wasn't as though I'd gone with an industrial company. Basically, my change just involved doing a whole lot of listening and trying to see what's going on."

Jim's relaxed attitude makes his job seem easy. But, of course, a position as CEO of an international company like American Express is in fact never easy. Jim is described by one who works with him as "a fierce competitor, who is not only brilliant, but has a vast supply of energy." He arrives at his office at 6:45 A.M. When he leaves around 7:00 P.M., he takes work home. "There's no point looking out the car window on my way home," he says. "I might as well be working."

Jim also takes work home on weekends; but, he protests, "I'm not a total workaholic. I do play golf, and I ski on occasion. I'm what you'd call a neo-workaholic. One of my father's favorite sayings was 'Work hard and play hard.' I'm a great believer in that philosophy.

"Yes, I do work long hours. I think anyone who's involved in the business world at a senior level has to. But as far as I'm concerned, it's as much avocation as occupation. There really aren't very many things I'd rather be doing than what I do here." It's no secret that not many people have this kind of enthusiasm for their jobs. Jim adds, "I'd say, if you don't enjoy your work, I think you ought to take another look around."

Because American Express is multinational, Jim spends a great deal of his time visiting different company locations around the world. In addition, he spends many evenings at community and civic functions. For a young CEO with a growing family, this kind of hectic schedule has presented a real challenge. The Robinsons have always made a point of taking family vacations; a favorite spot is Sun Valley. And when the children were young, Jim says, "I'd be home for dinner whenever I could manage it." He agrees that his career has required certain trade-offs and limited his time with his family. The long hours and travel are a predictable part of his job, he points out with a shrug. "It comes with the territory."

Despite the limitations on his time, Jim is involved in numerous civic activities. One particular interest is Memorial Sloan-Kettering Cancer Center, where he is a member of the Board of Managers. Another favorite cause is fund-raising for Spelman College, a school in Atlanta whose student body comprises predominantly black women. He points out, however, that he is frequently asked to work for good causes, and that it is often necessary to say no, recognizing that his prime responsibility is to American Express. Still it is important to him to find time—often on evenings and weekends—for such causes. "My father deeply believed," he explains, "that each of us should leave the world a little better than we found it. And I share that belief."

Jim seems to thrive on the pressures of his job. His desk is full but organized, and he is obviously relaxed as he sits back in his paneled office. From his window, the Statue of Liberty and Governors Island are visible, as are the East and Hudson rivers. He looks meditatively at photographs of his wife and children on a bookshelf opposite his desk and says, "The more pressure, the more interesting life is. It gets back to enjoying what you're doing. If you like your work, the more demands and challenges come with it, the more interesting it is. In fact, it builds up a sort of kinetic energy."

Jim also believes in challenging his co-workers in what he refers to as "constructive conflict." But he cautions that the emphasis is on the word "constructive."

"In an organization this size," he explains, "we bring together many competent people with different backgrounds and experiences, and we get them to interact. When it is done effectively in a fact-oriented fashion, the intellectual challenge brings out the best decisions the group can offer. This isn't necessarily easy. You have to get the kind of dialogue going that encourages people to speak up and then to fight for their point of view. And you have to orchestrate it so that it doesn't break into open warfare or go underground and become political—which is the worst thing in the world for an organization. If you can do all that, you have constructive and creative conflict.

"I would caution, however, that you must avoid an endless series of meetings, and you also have to avoid putting responsibility into a committee. You've got to place accountability and responsibility in the hands of a single individual. That person can use the committee as a source of input, but it must be clear that he is the one making the decision, within whatever boundaries of authority he has. With a committee decision, you don't know who made it, and you don't know who's accountable. So when something goes wrong, you don't know who's going to fix it!"

As Jim sees it, one of the most important functions of management at a large corporation is to involve a variety of people with different backgrounds in decision-making. Encouraging creativity, in the face of the fact that some parts of a large financial institution must operate with a high degree of precision and teamwork, can be especially demanding on a manager. "Creative people are great conceptualists," he says, "and they may tend to move too quickly without thinking through the implications. You certainly don't want to bind them up in the planning process and stifle the very thing you're trying to create. You can't expect everyone to operate with the same style, the same techniques. And hopefully you can be intelligent enough not to try to force all your people into the same mold. But in a big organization, you're going to have to have some form of discipline that the creative person has to accommodate to."

A strong believer in good communications within a company, Jim makes a point of getting out and talking to American Express people at every level. "I also make myself as approachable as my schedule will allow," he says. "This personal contact is vital. I not only do it when I can, I encourage all my associates to do it too."

One way American Express keeps the lines of communication open within the company is through a video news magazine called *On-Location*. The program visits different field locations and relays information about the company and its people to all employees of American Express and its subsidiaries. Recently Jim and Vice Chairman Alva Way met with a group of employees in the Amex Plaza cafeteria, where a spontaneous forum was filmed by *On-Location.*

One question of special concern dealt with the possibility of future automation: "What will the company's posture be toward those employees displaced by this technological evolution?"

In part, Jim's reply was "We are a growth company, as you know, and we've got to gain the productivity benefits that can only come with the utilization of technology. So I see it not as a displacement, but really as an opportunity to take advantage of the business that is going to be coming our way. . . . It clearly means that we're going to have to have the training capacity to make available to those people whose jobs are directly impacted the techniques, the knowledge, the wherewithal to move with that new breed of sophistication. And we'll be working very hard to do that." He also concurs with Al Way's suggestion that the personnel problem of the future is likely to be one of a shortage of people rather than a shortage of jobs.

In regard to the impact of technological advancement on American Express employees, Jim points out that already about 50 percent of the work force is employed in data processing and systems-related jobs. "We're usually identified as a diversified financial services company," he explains. "But I perceive us as a worldwide data processing and communications organization, using a broad definition of communications organization. We handle millions of transactions, many in an on-line real-time mode. There's Warner Amex Cable Communications, Inc. We've just acquired *International Food and Wine Magazine;* we already owned *Travel and Leisure* magazine.

Warner Amex Cable Communications, Inc., was formerly the cable television subsidiary of Warner Communications, Inc. In 1979, American Express made a $175 million acquisition of a 50 percent share in the cable company. The renamed company is one of the largest in the nation, servicing about 700,000 viewers through 143 cable systems in 29 states. One

unique feature of Warner Amex is the QUBE system in Columbus, Ohio—the only major interactive two-way cable system
in the country. Through use of in-home computer terminals,
QUBE permits viewers to "talk back"—to shop, register opinions on public issues, and countless other possibilities, all in
addition to the large variety of programming brought in by
cable. QUBE has been so successful that plans call for systems
to be installed soon in Houston, Pittsburgh, and Cincinnati
suburbs.

"We believe there's tremendous potential in QUBE," Jim
says. "We're very excited about it. Imagine the opportunity
to work with banks to offer banking services. And then there's
the potential for shopping from the home! We're already in
the direct mail business, and we see QUBE as a future extension
of the normal selling network. Our slogan now is 'Don't leave
home without us.' Maybe someday it will also be 'Don't *stay*
home without us.' "

American Express is aggressively seeking new markets in
this country. It has long been a household word around the
world because of its travel-related services. The American Express Card itself is accepted in over 150 countries; the company
processes more than 1 billion transactions each year! Traveler's
checks are issued at over 89,000 outlets across the globe. Obviously, tourism is a very big item for American Express, and
Jim points out that tourism is also very big business in its
own right.

"Tourism is the second largest item in world trade. In the
early 1970s, some believed that it would have been the largest
in the world by the year 2000, but then oil prices put the
petroleum industry too far ahead. The total volume of domestic
and foreign sales related to tourism is in excess of $400 billion.
Furthermore, tourism is good business. It's resilient. It's resis-
tant to tension and strife, and so far it's proven relatively im-
mune to the business cycle. People still travel, good times or
bad. In fact, travel is no longer a luxury. For millions of people,
it is a staple of life; for many others it's a necessary part of
doing business."

The economic impact of tourism is often disguised, he explains, by the diversity of the businesses involved. Tourism-influenced businesses include airlines, hotels, and restaurants, as well as large sectors of the entertainment and leisure industries. "Take this country," Jim says. "In the majority of states, tourism is among the top three industries. The service sector alone will generate a positive balance of payments of $45 billion this year—that figure is greater than our deficit in the goods category. I don't think the public realizes how important the service sector, or the tourism industry as part of that group, is to our economic health."

The energetic CEO pauses for a moment and then gestures for emphasis. "I think the most important aspect of tourism is that it serves as a bridge. When citizens travel to different countries, whether they travel on business or on vacations, they meet their counterparts. They have the opportunity to see that the other side doesn't have horns. If they can bridge the language barriers, they learn that people of other nationalities also have families and aspirations—very similar to ours. Instead of sitting home harboring their suspicions and prejudices, people need to go out into the world and meet individuals of other nations. Let them try to understand something about the other people's cultural heritage, how they got where they are—and why. Let them develop an appreciation for other peoples. These bridges are essential if we are going to survive in a nuclear world. In the past, bringing people together was a nicety. In this day and age, it's an absolute necessity."

Economic internationalism, Jim believes, is another necessary factor for safe co-existence. His expression makes it clear that he approaches this issue with great intensity. "Clearly the best and safest world is one which recognizes and supports our economic interdependence. Any reappearance of economic nationalism is a major obstacle. And yet, in times of tension, when large segments of the economy are affected by unemployment, and when international competition heats up, the short-sighted solution emerges: trade barriers. Right now there is an increasing trend in Europe toward legislation restricting the flow of data across national boundaries; but data is an essential part of international commerce. This kind of thing is what I call an 'invisible barrier to invisible trade,' and it's a result, I believe, of our non-recognition of the service sector.

"Traditionally, the main focus in discussing world trade has been on goods. Can you sell your farm product in this country? Can you sell your computers? But the service sector is a very large portion of world trade: it includes such businesses as accounting, banking, insurance, advertising, and travel. When individual countries impose licensing requirements, work-permit laws, or regulations that require insurance to be obtained from a local company, it's a dangerous thing. Barriers of this sort can eventually preclude foreign industry from doing any business in that country at all.

"Let's face it, these barriers also lead to a loss for the consumer. I'm a great believer in the competitive system that continually brings pressure to improve products and services. Economic nationalism which cuts off competition is a real loss to the individual consumer in the long run. It's essential to keep local parochialism from constructing boundaries that restrict a foreign company's capacity to do business. International trade is a major contributor to the rising standard of living around the world.

"This brings up another issue I think is important, and that is an unimpeded flow of information and acceptance of payment devices in the international financial community. It's essential that a traveler be able to pay for goods and services easily and conveniently wherever he goes. Any nation which tries to restrict competition or service threatens its own market share. When payment systems are curtailed by private or public institutions, the freedom of people to travel to all nations is inhibited. Therefore we must have an environment that's unencumbered by red tape trade restrictions. Whatever form it takes, protectionism slows down the growth of trade and business. When that happens, nobody wins. Any apparent gains are going to be very short-lived."

Jim points out that efficient worldwide payment systems

are entirely possible with advances in modern technology. If an American Express cardholder wishes to purchase an airline ticket in Hong Kong, the company's authorization system in Phoenix can approve the purchase in six seconds. Traveler's check dispensing machines employ much of the latest electronic hardware; the technology of instant communication and on-line service is real. Messages and images that once took hours or days to circle the globe now take seconds. Noting that many people fear technology, Jim comments, "Technology itself is basically neutral. How we use it makes it good or bad. In the 1980s, will we be moving toward a world of increasing uniformity and authority, in which people will have less choice, less freedom, and less privacy? Or will we be moving in the other, more sensible direction? The choice is up to us.

"We can see now that by and large the period between 1945 and 1965 was a time of reasonable social unity. The breakdown of that unity took place during the late sixties and seventies, when the social and political consensus of America vanished. The mood and direction of the country changed. We have all been bewildered and often dismayed by the fragmentation that has taken place. However, I believe some of the more recent developments have been positive. First, we're seeing a movement away from big government to local government initiative. Second, we're seeing less regulation become a national priority. Third, there's the continuing rise of working women and the two-income family. On the other hand, changes of concern are the replacement of the Protestant work ethic by what has been called the 'society of entitlement'; the psychology of high inflation and its complex impact on standards of living; and a decline in the strength of the two-party system, along with the growth in special interest groups.

"If there's one common thread linking these trends, I believe it's the shift from a system that valued conformity to one in which we have a variety of alternatives. In other words, we've been moving toward a multiple-choice society. And I believe this is very positive. Individuals must have a series of choices if we are to have a free society. Now, the implications for business of this shift toward diversity are profound. It means, among other things, that the private sector will have to cope with a society that is even more segmented by market than in the past. The tastes and values of the consumer will reflect great diversity, and diversity will represent new opportunities for those with the capacity to respond and deliver.

"I believe another important factor in the economics of the future is the shift toward a kind of me'ism, where people want their experience now. 'I'll worry about tomorrow when tomorrow gets here.' In some instances, there's nothing wrong with this attitude; in other cases, it's not so good. But regardless of how we may feel about it, it's definitely happening. We see it especially in the young people—the baby-boom children, who will become one-third of the adult population in the eighties. With annual incomes estimated at over $35,000, they will dominate consumer spending. This generation is less committed than previous generations to thrift, to investing in material possessions, and to building future security. Many value immediate pleasures—living well in the present and exploring a variety of personal experiences *now*. They feel *entitled* to 'intangible experiences' such as travel and entertainment. They feel entitled to personal career options that will enable them to afford these experiences.

"In the society of entitlement, everyone from conservationists to minority groups, from young to old, will feel it is his *right* to be heard, and it is the duty of business and government to respond. Increasingly, consumer wants will become needs, and needs will become demands. Quality-of-life expectations will continue to rise. Value will be of the utmost importance. In that environment, responsiveness to the consumer will be paramount to the success of a business.

"At American Express, we think a number of these trends will benefit our growth potential. Regardless of demographics or income levels, whether it's the search for a new experience, education and entertainment at home through cable, travel to Mozambique, or an evening at a good restaurant, we've got the products to serve these needs. All of these things fit into the trend to broaden one's life-style and experience base in the multiple-choice society."

Jim stresses that the new consumers will demand better service and higher quality than consumers demanded in the past. "At American Express," he says, "we're dealing with a traveler who is smarter, more demanding, and more sophisticated. He cannot be treated like the traveler of yesteryear. Advertising will pull people into our offices, but only efficient, convenient, personalized service will bring them back time and again."

The multiple-choice society raises a challenge for the American Express Travel Service, which now extends to 126 nations. Airline deregulation, changing rate structures, scheduling alternatives, and increased volume of business all make the job of the travel agent more demanding than in the past. "It will be a tremendous challenge to make travel manageable and satisfying," Jim says. After pausing a moment to collect his thoughts, he adds, "The answer to these challenges lies in the close coordination of our worldwide network of offices. We handle more than a billion transactions a year, but we're still a people business, and we still handle one person at a time.

"With travel as complex as it has become, we've got an immense number of opportunities to upset the customer, so we put a good deal of time and effort into training our people to be polite and customer-sensitive. 'No matter how good you are today, you can always be better tomorrow.' This is the message we're constantly driving home to the people in our travel offices. We tell the same thing to the people on our telephones who answer inquiries concerning lost cards or statements. These are just a few of the areas where we come in contact with the public; and we are fully aware that if we don't do this job well on a one-by-one basis, we don't have a business."

Because of the high visibility of American Express cards, traveler's checks, and the growing Travel Service, many people associate American Express only with these services. In 1968, however, the company expanded into another area of financial services when it acquired Fireman's Fund Insurance Company. Fireman's Fund is the nation's sixth largest insurer of home owners, and the eighth largest property-liability insurer in terms of premiums written. The company generated $2.7 billion revenue in 1979, with a net income of $186 million.

Jim points out that Fireman's Fund fits in very nicely with other American Express services. "All of our businesses are built on integrity—the ability to execute and the ability to perform," he explains. "If you go back to the great San Francisco fire, you'll find that at a time when many insurance companies failed to meet their obligations, Fireman's Fund performed. And, of course, there are some natural ways for the life insurance company to work together with the other divisions. For instance, we may offer a Fireman's Fund insurance policy to a customer scheduling a trip through our Travel Service. So insurance actually ties in very nicely with our other business."

If Jim continues at the helm of this gigantic diversified company until age sixty-five, he will have been American Express's chief executive for twenty-three years. Although he has no intention of thinking about retirement yet, he does comment that he hardly expects that long a tenure. "The life cycle of a chief executive officer in the 1980s and beyond," he says, "is probably going to be in the ten- to fifteen-year range, except where a policy of mandatory retirement at sixty-five shortens that.

"But as far as I'm concerned, the pressures and complexities of this job, the demands on you, are so great that you've just about had it by then. And there's another important consideration, too. In my opinion, your primary job as chief executive is to build a management team that can do the job better tomorrow than you are doing it today. And if you haven't managed to do that in ten years or so, you've failed to do your job."

10

Irving S. Shapiro

CHAIRMAN OF THE BOARD AND CHIEF EXECUTIVE
OFFICER,
E.I. DU PONT DE NEMOURS & COMPANY

Irving S. Shapiro joined Du Pont in 1951 as an attorney in the Legal Department. He played a major role in the antitrust case of the 1950s and early 1960s which forced Du Pont to divest itself of General Motors stock. In 1965, he was appointed assistant general counsel of the company. He became a vice president, director, and member of the Executive Committee in September 1970 and was designated a senior vice president in January 1972. On July 16, 1973, he was named vice chairman of the board, a new position which made him the second ranking officer of the company. Effective January 1, 1974, he became chairman of the Executive Committee, chairman of the board, and a member of the Finance Committee. He is also chairman of the company's Public Affairs Committee, an arm of the Executive Committee, which recommends company policies on important public issues and provides counsel on civic and governmental affairs.

From 1943 to 1951, Irv worked for the Justice Department and specialized in practice before the Supreme Court and the various circuit courts of appeal. Prior to joining the Justice Department, he worked for eighteen months at the Office of Price Administration in Washington, helping to establish a rationing program when the United States entered World War II.

Irv is a director of International Business Machines, Citibank and Citicorp, the Bank of Delaware, Continental American Life Insurance Company, and the Greater Wilmington Development Council.

He is a member of the Board of Directors of the Associates of the Graduate School of Business Administration of Harvard University, the Visiting Committee of the John F. Kennedy School of Government of Harvard University, the Board of Trustees of the University of Pennsylvania, and the Board of Governors of the University of Pennsylvania Law School.

Irv is an American director of the U.S.-U.S.S.R. Trade and Economic Council, Inc., and a member of the Advisory Council on Japan-U.S. Economic Relations. He is a founding member and a member of the Board of Governors of the Jerusalem Institute of Management in Jerusalem, Israel.

He is a trustee of the Conference Board and the Ford Foundation. He was elected chairman of the Business Roundtable in June 1976 and served in that capacity for two years. He was a vice chairman of the Business Council from January 1977 through December 1978. He is a trustee of the Academy of Natural Sciences, a member of the American Academy of Arts and Sciences, the Business and Professional Friends Committee of the National Center for State Courts, and the American Philosophical Society.

Irv was born July 15, 1916, in Minneapolis, Minnesota, the oldest of three sons of Lithuanian immigrants. He was graduated from the University of Minnesota with a bachelor of science degree in 1939 and received his bachelor of laws degree from the same university in 1941. The same year, he was admitted to the bar in Minnesota, and in 1944 he was admitted to practice before the United States Supreme Court. He was admitted to the Delaware bar in 1958.

He and his wife, Charlotte, live in Greenville, Delaware. Their son, Stuart, is an attorney in New York, and their daughter, Elizabeth, is a legal secretary in Wilmington.

When Irving Shapiro became chairman of the board and chief executive officer of the Du Pont Company in 1974, he was the second individual without Du Pont family ties ever to head the company. As a lawyer, he was also the first Du Pont CEO of modern times to have other than a technical or scientific education. The announcement that he would head the largest chemical company in the world surprised the entire business world. But perhaps nobody was more shocked than Irv himself.

The distinguished executive smiles as he recalls how he took the news that he was chosen to become Du Pont's thirteenth CEO. "Charles B. McCoy, my predecessor, had called my office on Friday, and since I was away, left a message for me to return the call the following Monday. Then on Monday he was tied up, so we finally arranged to meet later that week. When we did, we chatted for a while, and then he began talking about his personal plans for retirement. He casually added that he wanted to propose me as his successor.

"I was so surprised that I thought I had misunderstood him. But he continued to talk, giving me the specifics, so I asked him for a pad and pencil. I told him I wanted to take notes, and that's what I did. When he was done, I said, 'Do you mind if I read this back to you, sir? I want to make sure I understood you.' He told me to go ahead, and I did, and he confirmed that I had heard him right. Then he asked me, 'Are you willing to assume this position?'

"I answered that I regarded it as a great opportunity, which it obviously is, but that I wasn't sure I had the skills to do the job. However, I told him that if he had the confidence in me, I would give it a try."

Today Irv remains keenly aware of how difficult it is to predict what a person will do in the position of CEO. "You look for all kinds of indications," he says, "but no one can really determine how well a man will do until he's in the job. And if you're looking toward that position yourself, you can theorize and speculate; but until you're sitting right here with the problems coming in and you're resolving them, you just don't know whether you've got that flair or not. The answers are easy when you stand on the sidelines. But they're quite different when you have the responsibility and you have to live with your mistakes."

When he became Du Pont's CEO, Irv surpassed his own ambitions, which were originally confined to the field of law. By living at home and borrowing two hundred dollars a year, he completed his studies at the University of Minnesota Law School, and graduated in 1941. That fall, he started his own law firm, practicing tax law in Minneapolis. Soon after Pearl Harbor day, however, he received an emergency summons from Washington to help set up the Office of Price Administration, and by January 1942 he was in Washington. A year and a half later he transferred to the Criminal Division of the Department of Justice.

While Irv was at the Justice Department, his boss, Oscar Provost, was hired by Du Pont's Legal Department. About six years later, Irv was in New York City arguing a long case that was newsworthy enough to be written up in the *New York Times*. To his surprise, he received a phone call from Oscar Provost, who was in town on a business trip and had seen the article. The two met for lunch, and the luncheon

Fabian Bachrach

IRVING S. SHAPIRO

ultimately resulted in an offer to Irv to join the Legal Department at Du Pont. At thirty-five, Irv had been in Washington ten years, and seemed to have gone as far as he could in the Justice Department. "Furthermore," he comments, smiling, "Du Pont offered me two thousand a year more, and in those days that looked like a lot of money.

"As far as my goals at that time," he reflects, "I suppose I ultimately evolved an ambition to become general counsel—which, by the way, I never achieved. I certainly didn't think beyond the Legal Department during my first years. Given the history of the company, that would have been foolish."

A great deal of Irv's motivation, he emphasizes, has always come from the high quality of the people he works with. He considers himself fortunate in that, as a young lawyer, he entered a world of outstanding and brilliant individuals. "It was a whole new world I hadn't realized existed. I wanted to get into that world, and I started reaching. Right away I found out that all those brilliant guys got there because they worked hard. They were painstaking. Sure, they had better judgment than some other people. But the main thing was that they simply worked harder at it than the others."

By 1965, Irv had reached the highest position within the Legal Department that he would hold—assistant general counsel. Then in September 1970, he was named a vice president and became a member of the Executive Committee—the first individual from the Legal Department ever to move beyond it. In this capacity, Irv handled special projects for Charles McCoy, Du Pont's CEO. He was also liaison adviser for one fo the company's Industrial departments, and had similar responsibilities for liaison relationships with the Legal and Public Relations departments.

When Irv became CEO, he had been on the Executive Committee less than four years; most of his career had been spent in law. Naturally, he has been asked, "How in the world can an attorney head the world's largest chemical company—a highly complex industrial firm?"

"To tell the truth, I was worried about the same thing at

first," Irv candidly replies. "But I soon realized that everything I had done as a lawyer had really prepared me for this position. A good lawyer knows how to work with facts. He must sift out the essential from the non-essential; he must make judgments based on all the relevant considerations. Well, that's what the job is all about. I don't have to know technology. We've got plenty of Ph.D's around here who can educate me on technology when I need to know it. What I have to have—what anybody in this job has to have—is the ability to make sure I've got the right facts, and to know which ones are important and which are irrelevant. Then I need the judgment to see those facts just a little bit differently than anybody else sees them."

What does Irv believe to be the best background for a CEO? "By the time you get to filling a job of this kind," he answers, "the educational background is not particularly important. What really matters is the individual's experience, the breadth of his vision and judgment, his wisdom and ability to work with other people. Considerations of background are really secondary."

Irv is also careful to emphasize that a CEO does not work alone. "I think the best advice I could give to someone about to step into this position," he states modestly, "is 'Surround yourself with people who are brighter than you are!' That's just fundamental. If you've got any sense at all, you recognize it. No single person could do this job. And your best protection against serious errors is to make sure that the people around you are smarter than you are."

Because he has the right people around him, Irv doesn't have to be an expert in the technical aspects of research and development at Du Pont. In fact, one senior vice president is designated as Irv's "right arm" for all R & D activities. When Irv has to know something, this vice president can come in with the experts and answer the question in ABC language. "In effect," Irv says, "he'll tell me, 'This is what it comes down to. Here are the alternatives. Here are the risks. Here is the recommendation.' Then it's my option whether to accept the recommendation or reject it. When you have a liaison system like this, it's really not that complicated."

However, Irv cautions, that's not the same thing as saying that a CEO can move freely between industries and apply his skills to running any kind of company. "One good lesson I've learned from my experiences is that you can be good in your own industry and not nearly as good in somebody else's. It's not just a question of bringing certain skills to bear on the job, certain machinery. You must have the background, the understanding, the intuition that come with experience in a particular field. It's not all transferable."

In fact, Irv points out, the majority of corporations go to a great deal of trouble to develop leadership in-house. "When they do go outside for a chairman," he adds, "it's only because they have no alternative. They don't have people in-house whom they're prepared to go with. Now, at Du Pont, we've got more people capable of holding my job than there is time for them to achieve it. Any of the other five members of our Executive Committee is capable of holding this job, as are some of our department heads. Our great strength is our personnel—the human talent."

In January 1974, when Irv became CEO, the United States was in its worst recession since the Great Depression. Irv readily admits that his first year on the job was a trying one. "Sure, I made my fair share of mistakes that first year," he says matter-of-factly. "And I had to worry whether what was happening to the business was all attributable to the recession, or whether poor management was a factor. The challenge was 'Am I in the right job, and am I doing the best that can be done?'

"The doubt naturally cast a shadow at the beginning," he continues. "Under the best of circumstances, when you go into a new job, a new activity, you've got a period of uncertainty until you prove yourself. And in my case, the deep recession intensified my doubts. But once we got our problems under control and started achieving some success, those doubts disappeared."

Under Irv's leadership, Du Pont's sales rose from $5.9 billion in 1973 to $13.7 billion in 1980. In the same period, net earnings rose from $586 million to $716 million. Despite the concerns of his first year, Irv had adjusted very well to his position as CEO. His description of the capable individuals who head America's great corporations might well fit himself: "All the strong, exceptional companies build their people from within the organization. And by the time a man survives that race over the years, the odds are he's good. The system filters out weaknesses. If people don't have the strength, one way or another it separates them out."

The energetic executive points out that most CEOs have also gone through a rigorous selection process before assuming the top position. "The process favors individuals with character," he emphasizes, "people who possess both wisdom and judgment. They are also people with a sincere interest in doing what's best for their company. This is important, because it might be tempting to a CEO to make decisions which made his short-term performance look good while sacrificing long-term gains. For instance, Du Pont spent around $500 million in R and D during 1980, so if I gave the order to cut that to $250 million, our earnings would suddenly take a spurt. But in the chemical business, nearly every decision has to be made with long-term goals in mind. It takes three to four years to build a plant; and new technology may take ten to twenty years to mature.

"So it's imperative for a CEO to recognize that his own job is for a relatively short-term period, and his real responsibility is to make sure his successor doesn't find the cupboard bare. My predecessor did that for me," Irv says with a gesture, "and I spend a good part of my time making sure that the decisions I make will leave this office in good shape for my successor."

After a brief pause, Irv points out that a CEO does not have quite the capacity for independent action that some people might imagine. "In all companies," he explains, "the chief executive has a board that's looking over his shoulder and holding him accountable. If he tried to play the game of creating short-term gains that would make him look good but would hurt the company years from now, the directors would soon raise the question, 'Are you doing the right thing?' So he'd be held accountable. But if the selection process has worked properly, the person in the job knows better than to play the game that way, in any case."

In making his decisions, Irv places a great deal of value on the feedback from those around him. "Part of this feedback comes through the grapevine," he explains, "and through relationships you've built up over the years. Part of it comes through your colleagues. Whomever you're talking to, the trick is to ask the right questions and pay close attention to the answers you get. It's simply a matter of continually asking different people, 'What's your reaction?' 'What's going on?'

"The great secret," he continues, "is to have really capable people around you. But their ability is not useful to you if they don't feel comfortable letting you know exactly what they think. I've told the people I work with that part of their job is to save me from my own mistakes. And here at Du Pont we've created a climate in which employees know they're not expected to be yes-men. I believe it's essential to a CEO that his key people understand that they're expected to be straightforward, and they're not going to be penalized for bringing bad news. I've applauded colleagues who have told me, 'Look, you're off the track, and if you do this you're apt to make a mistake.' Some of them say it very directly, and others say it more subtly. However they do it, this is what I need. I'm going to make my share of mistakes in any event, but I can avoid some of them if I get good advice from my colleagues."

Because this is true, Irv believes that the first thing every CEO must know is that "this is *not* an ego trip. You can't afford to let your ego get in the way of job performance," he stresses. "You've got to be honest with yourself and recognize that you're going to make your share of mistakes—no matter what. So you'd better learn how to live with those mistakes, and avoid repeating them. But to keep mistakes to a minimum, you've got to have capable people around—they save you from yourself!"

Irv's feeling about capable people reflects overall policy at Du Pont. It has long been a company practice to reward employees for outstanding achievements. In some cases, if an employee develops an idea and pushes it to a successful conclusion, the employee is given a special reward in the form of cash or company stock. A classic example occurred in the 1930s, when a young marketing man became interested in methanol, an ordinary garden variety liquid chemical, which sold then for fifty cents a gallon. The employee suggested that the company put methanol in a can with an inhibitor and sell it as an anti-freeze for $1.50 a gallon. As Irv explains it, "His management kept telling him he was way off base, but they let him do it because he was so insistent. That concept made a lot of money for Du Pont, and he was well rewarded. That kind of creative persistence is what we strive to encourage."

Although Du Pont is very modern in its incentive plans, historians claim that a pioneering spirit still exists in the huge company, a spirit similar to that of Éleuthère Irénée du Pont de Nemours, who founded the company in 1802. Originally established as a high-quality gunpowder mill, the company supplied much of the United States military gunpowder requirements during the War of 1812. Later, Du Pont played a major role in supplying gunpowder to the Union Army during the Civil War. In World War I, the company supplied more than 40 percent of the gunpowder used by the Allies.

At the turn of the century, however, the company had begun to diversify, building plants to manufacture dyes and organic chemicals. By the 1920s, Du Pont was venturing into such products as cellophane and nitrocellulose. The former revolutionized packaging, while the latter found early use in movie and X-ray films. Next came neoprene, plastics, and other manmade materials. By the 1930s, the company had developed sophisticated plastics such as Lucite (acrylic resin). The next decade brought Teflon (fluorocarbon resin), polyethylene (a plastic destined to become a high volume product), and Orlon (acrylic fiber). New Du Pont products launched during the 1950s included Dacron polyester fiber and many agricultural chemicals.

The list of new Du Pont products, the result of the company's commitment to extensive research and development, is one of the most impressive in the annals of business and industry. Contributions made during the 1960s and 1970s alone are too numerous to name. Nevertheless, the giant corporation maintains the family atmosphere of its early days. The pride its army of employees has in the Du Pont achievement can be sensed at its world headquarters in Wilmington, Delaware.

The annual reports attest to the fact that Du Pont has continued to grow and prosper under Irv's leadership. Yet his influence has also extended to an arena beyond the corporate world. During the 1970s, a new breed of corporate chiefs evolved: managers with a highly developed concern for social and political issues, who are involved in developing a positive and effective relationship between business and government. They know that no company is an island; none can prosper for long if the country is unsound. Within this inner circle, no business leader has been more active than Irv. In a select fraternity of influential business figures, he has taken a leadership role and has helped redefine the job descriptions of CEOs for future generations.

Irv has the special commitment to his country sometimes found in the children of immigrants. Lithuanian by birth, his father was a pants presser and his mother a sweatshop garment worker. In his rise to the position of CEO, Irv is a shining example of the working out of the American Dream. It is typical of him that he explains his social leadership by saying simply, "I always wanted to make sure I didn't take more from the system than I was putting back."

As a past chairman of the Business Roundtable, Irv appears to spend as much time in Washington as in Wilmington, working with the belief that "business and labor and government will have to come together to solve many of the nation's socioeconomic problems." He believes that the business leaders of the 1980s and '90s will follow in the footsteps of his generation of CEOs, many of whom have devoted a significant portion of their time to such activities. "It's startling how much corporate America has changed," he points out. "In the past, businessmen wore blinders. After hours, they would run to their clubs, play golf with other businessmen, have a martini—and that was about it. They did not see their role as being concerned with public policy issues.

"In a world where government simply took taxes from you and did not interfere with your operations, maybe that idea was sensible. In today's world, it is not. I'm much more interested in what Russell Long thinks than what some businessman thinks. And you can find out from Russell Long very simply what he thinks." The robust five-foot-nine executive grins briefly and then continues. "I'm confident that most corporation chiefs today understand the outside world, and can deal with policy issues in America and abroad. I know if I were choosing a CEO, I would not be overly concerned with his education or specific background. I would ask how he relates to the larger world. Does he understand policy issues? Or is he a person who knows how to produce widgets but can't do anything else?"

Irv views his own role as CEO of the world's largest chemical company as a "quasi-public job." He emphasizes that his job description includes more than just being in the office and performing traditional functions. "In this capacity, you must relate to the various constituencies at Du Pont, and also to government, to public policy issues, and so on. Of course, to do that, you have to have associates who can carry out a fair amount of the internal job. Secondly, you have to work hard. If I spend a day at the Ford Foundation in New York, as I will tomorrow, I have to make up for it over the weekend, doing the work that I won't get done at the office. It's that simple."

Irv believes that the sacrifice is well worth making, and that, as a result, his generation of management has laid the foundation for a new role for business in society. He predicts better and more effective cooperation between business and government in the years to come. In fact, he states, "As American business becomes even more internationalized, I suspect that competition will force us to move closer to the patterns of government-business cooperation which exist in some other countries. This does not mean government passivity or compliance. I do not think you could call the governments of West Germany or Japan anyone's weak sisters. It does mean that government will not approach business as its sworn enemy. Even an arm's-length relationship will allow us to shake hands now and then."

Like Irv, the new generation of management to which he refers will carry a heavy work load. Extracurricular activities away from the executive suite will demand dedication and add long hours of work to already hectic schedules. "There's no question about it," Irv says, "it calls for family cooperation and sacrifice. But in my case, this has been true throughout my entire career, not just when I became CEO. As a young attorney, I had one case assignment that required me to be in New York for a year and a half. My family lived in Washington, and I commuted home every other weekend.

"What it boils down to is a question of objectives. If you decide this is the way you want to play it, and your wife and children agree, you can make it work. On the other hand, if it's 'just a job,' then it will never work. Trade-offs are part of life, and you have to recognize that. My daughter Elizabeth, our youngest child, was two years old before I really got to know her. Now, I wouldn't urge that as a way to live. On the other hand, there are times when a person has to make that kind of accommodation in order to achieve. And my children have benefited from the price they paid. Their lives are a little better because of the sacrifices. But life isn't a bowl of cherries. You do have to make adjustments and sacrifices. However, isn't this true for the guy in the plant? There are times when the plant isn't running well, and he's there for eighteen hours. His kids don't see him, either!"

On a typical day, Irv is at the office from eight in the morning until around six, when he leaves with a full briefcase. Most weekday evenings involve some kind of business activity. Weekends are what Irv calls "study periods." Leaning back in his chair, he explains. "During the weekends, I study the longer reports. Those are the materials that will come before the Executive Committee the following week. That's also when I catch up on all those things I wanted to do during the week but didn't get done. It's my clean-up period. This is a seven-day-a-week job."

Nevertheless, Irv is obviously a relaxed and happy man. "Some people marvel at the energy I put into my work," he admits. "What they don't understand is that this is not a job in the sense of having to go to work. It's a great experience. You live for it. You're excited about it. You revel in the accomplishments, and you cry for the defeats. It's a part of your life. I'd much rather be doing what I'm doing than be out on the golf course—It's that simple. Now, that doesn't mean that I don't enjoy the golf course, but the fact is that I have more fun here. I'd rather be here than anyplace else. I felt that way about practicing law, too. My work represents a chance to accomplish things—to make things happen."

As Irv approaches retirement age, he is frequently asked about his plans for the time when he will no longer be running at a hundred miles an hour. "I have no intention of stopping work," he replies quickly. "When I look around, I see that people who have active lives and do things seem to live longer, and are much happier. It's not a question of the money, but of being productive and doing something with your life that's worthwhile. The idea of going home with my pension and just playing golf every day is the worst thing I can think of.

"I have three options before me," he reflects. "I can remain in the business world, go back to law, or go into government. I'm in the happy position of being able to choose among the three. But it's something I won't decide until I actually retire."

With his strong interest in public policy, Irv is one of the 1970s generation of CEOs who serve as role models for younger managers. Du Pont is a forerunner among companies that encourage their people to become politically active. Du Pont employees who serve in appointive or elective offices on the local, state, or national level may spend up to 20 percent of their working time on those activities—on the house. "We believe," Irv explains, "that with exposure in the outside world, they become better employees. And we know they've got a contribution to make." Du Pont managers have never had a problem accepting the active involvement in public affairs which is expected of them, because they understand that it is part of the job description.

If the CEO is in Washington, some people may ask, who's minding the store? Irv insists that there really is no conflict between building your business and dealing with public policy questions. "The two go hand in hand. The most successful businesses are located in good communities with good schools, good libraries, good everything. I think you'll find that the men running successful businesses are also the men who are bringing their talent to bear on public policy issues. Obviously, you can't ignore the responsibilities of running the business to concentrate only on doing good. For one thing, if you don't make money in your business, you can't afford to do these things. You have to be selective. And you have to measure what you're doing, so you don't divert your time uselessly. But there's no reason to argue that unless you devote eighteen hours a day to your business, you're not doing your job. That shows a very narrow concept of business."

Irv himself feels it's part of his job to make sure there's a decent educational system in New Castle County, Delaware. Supporting legitimate theater, which contributes to an attractive cultural atmosphere, is also an extension of his responsibility. In general, he believes a better quality of life for the community will benefit Du Pont by helping the company attract good people to the area. In the process, the entire community of Wilmington benefits. "I'm aware of the fact that some people have criticized me for spending too much of my time on government problems," Irv says. "But I think the answer to that is that you cannot separate a business from the community and the nation. They are inseparable. You've got to deal with the whole thing."

For Irv, there is another question involved. "It's almost like a theology. It's a question of what your initial premises are. I, for one, think that there's a strong case for the idea that government, industry, and labor unions all exist to serve the public interest—not for private purposes as such. And unless they can demonstrate that that's what they're doing, they have no legitimacy. I don't limit this philosophy to industry. I say the same applies to the government. Unless government can demonstrate that it's really meeting the needs of the people, then something is wrong, and changes are in order."

Many business people have been concerned about the general lack of public support for business. Irv believes this will change as more and more business leaders take public stances on issues and become widely known. "The executive must be accessible to the press," Irv stresses. "If you look at the history of American businessmen, they've been essentially nameless and faceless. The public identifies corporate names, but they don't identify the ballplayers. I don't think you can get the necessary public support unless the public can see a person, identify with him, and understand what makes him tick. So I've been advocating for some time now the idea that top executives should get out where the public is, take positions, and let themselves be judged—let the public react.

"Now, I've found, by and large, that any group of people who know a businessman tend to like him. He's a very popular guy in his own town; but he's not very popular anyplace else—because they don't know him. Well, the way to solve this problem is to get him known, by letting the public see him doing things that serve the public interest.

"In the past, businessmen have been too timid about their public profile. They've been afraid to take the heat from the press, so they've lived essentially private lives. That might have been appropriate at one time in our history, but not today. Today they have to be accessible to the media."

Irving S. Shapiro is one business leader who is not timid about voicing his opinion, even on such controversial subjects as nuclear energy. Recently he addressed the National Petroleum Refiners Association on the subject, in a speech firmly in favor of nuclear power. "It seemed to me that the only voices being heard on the subject," he explains, "were those of people like Jane Fonda and Tom Hayden. Those people in the business who had the knowledge and experience were relatively quiet. Yes, the electrical power industry was trying to be heard, but they were seen as having a self-interest. I thought Du Pont was in a unique position. We were not directly in the business, yet we've had more experience with nuclear energy than anyone else in the world."

Du Pont has been running reactors and handling nuclear wastes since World War II, when the company built the Hanford, Washington, facility and then the Savannah River atomic plant in South Carolina (which it continues to operate for the government today for a fee of one dollar per year). The Savannah River plant site covers 315 square miles, and contains five nuclear reactors, three of which are in operation at present. These reactors are not designed to generate electricity but to produce nuclear materials for defense; they are comparable in scale, however, to reactors found in major power plants. Savannah River, with about eight thousand employees, has been in operation for twenty-six years—120 reactor years. During this period, Irv stresses, no member of the operating staff has suffered an injury from radiation. Furthermore, nobody in the surrounding area has been exposed to a radiation level of more than a few percentage points of the natural background radiation. "From a health standpoint," Irv says, "the most hazardous part of the plant is not the nuclear reactors but the coal-fired power station used to generate the electricity to run the facility."

The Savannah River location also stores and controls one of the largest accumulations of nuclear wastes in the country— 20 million gallons of radioactive wastes, stored in underground double-walled steel and concrete tanks. Agreeing that the handling of these wastes is a serious concern, Irv points out that we already have the technology to vitrify liquid waste and dispose of it permanently. Sophisticated processes make it possible to encapsulate this waste permanently into much smaller volume and then to store the containers deep underground, so that virtually all risk to the public is removed. If this process is used, a piece of glass approximately one quart in volume would contain the wastes generated by a year's consumption of electricity for a thousand people.

"There's no question that we have a great need for nuclear power," Irv emphasizes. "Nuclear plants should be capable of producing 20 to 25 percent of our electricity within the next ten to fifteen years, perhaps as much as 35 percent by the turn of the century—versus the 11 percent they presently produce. This would be prudent and safe, and the technology to make it happen already exists. Other nations are taking this route—more than forty of them—and unless the United States does the same, we may lose our position in nuclear technology."

Irv is acutely aware of the general public's fear of nuclear power. "People seem to have a vision of another Hiroshima," he comments, "or a disaster where the whole thing melts down and an entire community is wiped out. But that just can't happen. There is no experience which says the risk involves a million people. The risk boils down to something like Three Mile Island, where nobody was killed, nobody was injured, and nobody was damaged in any way." He points out that according to the Kemeny Commission report, the most radiation anyone absorbed was about as much as he might receive annually from dental and medical X rays, and "the chance that we will someday see an increase in the incidence of cancer because of that accident is so small as to be statistically meaningless."

One of Irv's primary reasons for advocating nuclear power is that he believes there is no good alternative. "The fact is," he maintains, "we don't have other power resources for energy, particularly electricity, other than coal. And if you get down to the choice between coal and nuclear energy, the nuclear option is much more attractive. In fact, more lives are lost in mining, transporting, and using coal than will ever be lost in building or maintaining nuclear power plants."

While he firmly believes in the safety of nuclear power, Irv acknowledges that the general public fears this option to such an extent that new plants for electrical power generation are not presently being authorized. "Nobody wants to put up the money. And it takes twelve to fourteen years in this country to get a facility built and licensed. So we've got to change our policies. The public has to be convinced that this development is beneficial.

"It's interesting to note that during World War II there was no problem building nuclear facilities—because they would help win the war. And I don't believe the people who object today would protest if there was a threat of invasion. They'd say, 'Our security is at stake. By all means, we've got to defend ourselves.' The fact is, the power issue may not be as dramatic as a threat of invasion, but it's every bit as important. If we can't generate enough electrical power to meet the needs of the country, the economy will slowly grind to a halt."

Irv feels that it is particularly appropriate for him, as head of Du Pont, to take a public stand on nuclear power. "We've had more experience with nuclear power than anybody," he says, "and it's been all good. We've never told the story publicly, and that's why I felt it was my obligation to make that speech. Everybody thought it was very risky, but it seemed perfectly straightforward to me to take the facts as facts and present them."

Although Irv has been a leading spokesman for the American business community during his tenure as CEO of Du Pont, employees describe him as "down to earth," and "very human." He is most often characterized as "a man with a great common touch." His office bears this out. Located on the ninth floor of the company's headquarters in downtown Wilmington, Delaware, it is the same relatively modest office Du Pont CEO's have occupied since 1905, when the building was constructed.

The windows look out on Market Street, the busy main shopping area, and on the Delaware River, whose banks are edged with several Du Pont plants.

The office is warmly furnished and paneled in mahogany. On the wall behind Irv's desk is a large oil portrait of three past CEO's—Pierre S. du Pont, who served from 1915 to 1919; Irénée du Pont, 1919 to 1926, and Lammot du Pont, 1926 to 1940. The almost life-size painting is a visible reminder of the company's family tradition—a tradition of warmth and community that continues to the present day. Irv is clearly proud of his place in this great tradition. Both his public actions and his words reveal his strong sense of altruism, as well as his unfaltering belief in American free enterprise.

Much of Irv's public work has stemmed from his concern for the American economic system, and his belief in the growing necessity of business-government cooperation. "We're the only nation I know of," he points out, "that has had an adversary relationship develop between industry and government over the past fifty years." He shakes his head. "In the other major nations, government and industry work very closely together. This is certainly true in Japan, and it's true in Germany. I've said many times that I have never seen Chancellor Helmut Schmidt fail to have both business and labor representatives in his party. Even when he entertains people at lunch, he has that mix. It's quite a different approach!

"If we're going to compete internationally, labor, industry, and government are going to have to work together to solve problems and establish policies that make sense in a competitive world. This doesn't mean that government should turn over its responsibility to either industry or labor. What I'm suggesting is that government, industry, and labor work *together* in developing policies that make sense for the nation as a whole."

According to Irv, the lack of cooperation between American government and industry is a major reason why non-U.S. firms have been growing twice as fast in sales as have American firms. He believes that government overregulation is one particularly dangerous result of poor business-government relations.

"While other nations have significant anti-trust laws and environmental programs, only in America is there such a variety of reviews, regulations, controls limits, and challenges thrown at big business. One of my predecessors, Crawford Greenewalt, said it best: 'In the United States we indict a businessman under the anti-trust laws for doing the things that in Great Britain he would be knighted for.' "

As an attorney, Irv is particularly intrigued by this problem. "Do you know," he asks, "that the only people in this country who deal with anti-trust are the lawyers? It's curious. Lawyers are supposed to interpret the law. But in the anti-trust field, they also make the economic decisions. However, in the training and education of a lawyer, there is nothing that qualifies him to make economic policy for the country. Nevertheless, when a young person fresh out of law school is put into the Anti-Trust Division, or the Federal Trade Commission staff, he suddenly thinks he's an expert on economic policy. This is something you don't find abroad. It's simply silly!"

As one of the nation's most active business leaders, Irv strongly believes government must promote capital investment and R & D. "The context is that the government has grown so large and demanding of industry, both in terms of regulation and in terms of taxation, that it has slowed down productivity. This is evident when you see what's happening in Japan, Germany, and most European countries. It translates into lower capital investment with reference to GNP in the United States than in other countries. This is a problem we've got to solve. I think the starting point has to be the realization that the public sector cannot consume so much of the productivity as it does now. Up until about 1973, around 18 percent of the GNP was going to the public sector. Now it's up to 23 percent. While that might not seem like much of a change, percentage wise, in terms of dollars it represents an enormous sum of capital. What that tells us is that we're consuming our capital rather than reinvesting it.

"We need to focus on increasing our productivity," he stresses. "That means we must build modern plants with new technology, so we can be competitive. It means we must invest in R and D to make sure that our technology for the eighties and nineties is different than it was in the seventies. These are important capital expenditures, and they must be made. But they can't be made if there isn't enough cash left in a business to do it. So we've got to change our system of taxation to encourage savings and investment. Enough of this encouragement of debt as a way of life! Then too, I think a reduction in the size of government is in order, so it can be better managed, and so it is not intervening in areas that don't call for government intervention, and could be better managed by local or individual decision.

"In a sense, I'm suggesting a governmental structure more like what we had a hundred years ago than what we have now. In those days, the states and cities had primary responsibility for their territory, and the federal government picked up the rest. We've simply turned it around. And it's grown so big that it cannot be managed. Anyone who thinks of the federal government in terms of designing a way to manage it will have to conclude that it is not being managed at all!"

As American director of the U.S.-U.S.S.R. Trade and Economic Council, Inc., Irv is well versed in the problems within the Russian system. "It's much worse in Russia, because the *only* structure in their society is government. All the VIPs are government officials. The bureaucracy, the rules, the regulations, the paperwork—why, it's simply overwhelming. To paraphrase an old Churchill line about democracy, 'It's got a lot of defects; it just happens to be better than anything else we can come up with.'

"But I think we could make our system of government work much better. The heart of the problem is a political system in which the people in public office want to promise every constituent group whatever they want—and our society can't produce enough wealth to do everything. But this can be overcome by good management. It's no different than running Du Pont. I can't invest more capital than I have, and I know that. We have to tailor our investment program to our capital and our borrowing capacity. And in government, you can't give away more than you've got without creating inflation and other serious consequences. As soon as the American people accept that premise and start putting heat on the politicians, as, for instance, the Germans have done, then we can lick inflation."

Irv is quick to agree that there are significant differences between business and government. "In the business world, we optimize; in the political world, we compromise. In business, you look for efficiency. The financial analysis tells you that if you do this, you will get these results; if you do that, you will get other results. At that point, a businessman makes a decision.

"But in the political world, that's just the beginning of the analysis. Then you ask, 'Where are the political pressures? What is the political interest? What are the constituency groups? How do you respond to everybody's aspirations?' And so you're always working out compromises. In business, your goals are more precise and measurable. Everybody in a company has the same objective. There may be some competition between groups in a company, for capital, for instance, but it's quite different than it is in the public sector, where compromise is the only way to make progress."

In his concern for the American economy, Irv Shapiro is in the best Du Pont tradition. The Du Pont Company has a long and illustrious history of working in the public interest, dating back to its manufacture of gunpowder during the War of 1812. Then, too, the company has poured billions of dollars into research and development. In 1980, Du Pont spent nearly $500 million on R & D, and, as Irv puts it, "We know right off the bat that it will not all be profitable. What we're gambling on is that one or two or maybe three projects will develop something genuinely new, and open up new fields of technology—perhaps come up with the answers to serious problems.

"I don't believe a company can think only in terms of profit. While I don't deny the profit motive, my view is that business is a means to an end—it isn't the end itself. Now, of course, a company must make money, or it can't do anything else. But if you visualize your role as one of simply making money, you're missing the whole point. The point of running a business is to solve problems society has—to provide jobs; to provide goods and services; to help create a better way of life."

Conclusion

In today's computerized world, the multinational corporation with its billions of dollars in assets often seems dehumanized. Giant corporations are identified as their products: "the airlines"; "the telephone company"; "the electric company." General Motors, General Electric, and Du Pont have come to represent automobiles, appliances, and chemicals—rather than people working together in a business enterprise. The "board" of a multinational company is seen as a faceless collective rather than a group of individuals. And the furthest removed, least identifiable force within the corporation often is its chief executive officer.

In the past, the CEO could maintain the image of an authoritative, mysterious force who rarely emerged from the executive suite. Today, however, the nation needs strong leadership—not only in the public sector but in the private sector as well. America's faith in the free enterprise system and in big business needs to be reinforced. For that reason, these CEO's have generously offered to share their stories and philosophies in this book.

The Chief Executive Officers was written to introduce Americans to the kind of people who run big business today. The men profiled here are representative of the quality and integrity of our country's chief executives. They demonstrate that we can be proud of American business, that our largest and most successful enterprises are headed by capable and conscientious people. Their stories also show that our giant corporations are structured in such a way that talent is not only permitted but encouraged to rise to the highest level.

The careers of the ten men profiled here illustrate that the American Dream is alive and well in the corporate world. The office of the chairman is open to anyone with ability, motivation, and conviction. With the exception of Ralph Lazarus, whose father chaired Federated Department Stores, and Jim Robinson, whose father headed a bank in Atlanta, each CEO began his career in true Horatio Alger style—and at the bottom of the corporate ladder. But even Ralph Lazarus didn't start as an executive; his first full-time job was as a piece goods salesman in the Lazarus department store. In fact, by the time he began his career in 1935, his family no longer had a controlling interest in the business. And Jim Robinson, the American Express CEO, did not step out of college into his father's bank. He entered Morgan Guaranty's training program and spent his first weeks "pushing those little black carts with securities up and down Broad Street" in Lower Manhattan.

Their stories also suggest that no company, whatever its tradition, is closed to new talent. Irving Shapiro's rise to the top position at Du Pont stunned the business world. A lawyer with no Du Pont family ties, Irv was elected to head the world's largest chemical company in 1973. Today he is one of the most respected business leaders in America.

At one time, the chief executive's office was virtually reserved for older men, and gaining it typically took thirty to forty years. Dick Ferris's story shows that age is no longer an essential criterion. After graduating from college in 1962, Dick began working as manager of the Olympic Grill for Western International's Seattle Hotel. In 1970, Western International was acquired by UAL, Inc. Four years later, at age thirty-eight, Dick was president of United Airlines. At forty-three, he was named CEO of the holding company UAL, Inc. Only in America can an individual move from managing a hotel restaurant to heading the nation's largest airline in twelve years.

Dick's experience indicates the commitment of modern business to encouraging talent wherever it is found within a company. Tom Murphy points out that General Motors vigorously attempts to give its executives the varied background and experience necessary to handle top management positions. He is one of several CEOs in this book who affirm something like "How comforting it is to be chairman and know that there are capable people in the wings who could lead this corporation, literally dozens of them with the talent and willingness to do a good job."

As young men beginning their careers, many of these CEOs did not aspire to their present positions. When he joined Avon, Dave Mitchell recalls, "I certainly wasn't thinking about someday being an executive. I was more interested in the present—I wanted a steady job!" Likewise, when Tom Murphy is asked whether he thought he would someday become CEO of General Motors, he answers, "Never! Never in my wildest dreams."

Other men had early and obvious ambitions. Jim Robinson believed in setting his targets high. He explains that when he joined American Express at age thirty-five, he did so with a clear objective in mind—"if not the office of CEO, then one of the top positions in the company. If you don't swing at 'em, you don't hit 'em." Bob Beck also had high ambitions. "It entered my mind very early on that I would like to be the CEO of Prudential," he admits. "Now, that's the kind of thing people are sometimes reluctant to say. However, I used to say it when I was young and new in the business." Bob's wife, Frances, shared his dream, and they worked together at it as a family.

Whatever his ambitions, each of these men always gave his full attention to his current position. None saw any particular job as merely a steppingstone to a higher position. Reg Jones believes that this capacity to devote oneself to the job at hand is vital to success. Reg himself almost refused a promotion to vice president of finance when GE offered it, because he was enjoying his job as group vice president of the Components and Construction Materials Group. "I've seen it happen where a person becomes so concerned about his *next* job that he's not putting real effort into his current job," Reg explains. "If you get yourself involved in what you're doing, and if you're proficient at it, the next job takes care of itself. Certainly it's important to have long-term goals; but they are achieved by concentrating on the job at hand."

Dick Ferris agrees that long-term goals are necessary, but adds, "What you want to concentrate on day by day is doing the job at hand to the best of your ability. Do it well, do it better than anyone else around you, and you don't have to worry about a thing. You'll stand out like a sore thumb, and pretty soon you'll be singled out for promotion. Because every company needs good people, so it's very easy to be recognized."

Like Reg and Dick, Charlie Brown concentrated on the job at hand. "I have never given much thought to where I would end up with this company," he says. "Of course, I always knew that the Bell System believes in developing its own people for higher positions. But I've been happy with the jobs I had, and it's been my objective to enjoy my present job and do well at it. It is absolutely not necessary to politick or step on anyone's neck to get ahead. Your results speak for themselves. You compete best by doing well at your job and proving your competence."

It's interesting to note that an individual can begin in any position within a corporation and move to the top. Tom Murphy began with General Motors in the accounting department. Irv Shapiro was an attorney. Bob Beck was a salesman. Charlie Brown had an engineering education, and Jim Robinson's background was in finance. Tom emphasizes that within GM, any individual from any specialty can move into general management. "I don't think any one background is better than another. While my predecessor, Dick Gerstenberg, was primarily a financial man like myself, others have had backgrounds in engineering, manufacturing, marketing, and other areas."

Reg Jones agrees that "it's not just the area in which you enter the company, but the effort you're willing to put forth." Irv Shapiro would not recommend any particular degree for a young person who aspired to be a CEO. "By the time you get to filling a job of this kind, the educational background is not particularly important. What really matters is the individual's experience, the breadth of his vision and judgment, his wisdom and ability to work with other people. Considerations of background are really secondary."

While educational background is not a major consideration, on-the-job training plays an important role in the development of a senior manager. Ralph Lazarus recalls working at the family department store when he was so young he had to stand on a crate to see over the counter. He believes that practical experience may be more important in retail than any other business. Ralph notes that young executives without adequate on-the-job training often fail because they have a "people blindness."

Jerry McAfee believes that his own early employment experience at Gulf has been valuable to him as a senior manager. First employed by the company as a summer laborer moving barrels, he remarks that there's no better way to learn to appreciate what it takes to get a job done than to have the actual experience. "When you've worked your share of graveyard shifts," he says, "it helps you understand what goes on out there."

Avon's Dave Mitchell says, "This is a field you don't learn in a classroom. You don't go to Harvard or Stanford to find out how to run a direct selling company." He explains that even MBAs recruited by the company are put through the ranks. "There just isn't any question about it. The day-to-day roll-up-the-sleeves get-in-there-and-fight approach is essential." Dave also feels that his own experience selling door-to-door to test new products has enhanced his ability to understand problems brought to him by Avon associates.

Similarly, Bob Beck values his early experiences as a life insurance agent. He still recalls his own slump, in which he was unable to make a sale for eight weeks, and he believes no other business experience has served him so well. "Every time I have worked with a struggling agent, I knew what it was like to be frustrated, lacking in confidence, totally shaken." As a result, Prudential agents talk about Bob's ability to relate to all agents, those who are having difficulty as well as the superstars. "He's been there," they say. "He's not isolated in an ivory tower."

The companies themselves are well aware of the value of varied experience to senior management, and attempt to provide that experience to talented young people. Charlie Brown, for instance, has held twenty-three positions within the Bell System during his thirty-four years at AT&T. Reg Jones explains that at GE, technical people are routinely put into training programs which give them the opportunity to work in different areas.

A common theme stressed by these CEOs is the importance of being "people-oriented." As American Express's Jim Robinson says, "We handle more than a billion transactions a year— but we're still a people business, and we still handle one person at a time. . . . We put a good deal of time and effort into training our people to be polite and customer-sensitive." Perhaps no one emphasized the importance of people in a business as strongly as Ralph Lazarus. In a retail business, he says, "the top management must be effective in supporting the people at every level, and they must be able to recognize enthusiasm, and be able to generate it . . . everything depends on the effectiveness of our people. The difference between our store and the competition is whatever the people make it. . . . We are a people business—and how we find our people, train them, handle them, and promote them will pretty much determine our future."

Far from being isolated in the executive suite, these CEOs stress the importance of communication with company employees. Jim Robinson communicates to the thousands of American Express employees through the company's video news magazine, *On-Location*. And he says, "I also make myself as approachable as my schedule will allow. This personal contact is vital. I not only do it when I can, I encourage others on my staff at the corporate level to do it." Dick Ferris also maintains an open door and talks to UAL employees whenever he has an opportunity; for instance, he conducts spontaneous rap sessions with pilots and other UAL employees when he is between flights at airports. He too stresses that "this is a people business, and we find time to communicate with our people. We make time to interact with them."

Typical of many chief executives, GE's Reg Jones spends a major amount of his time with people. He emphasizes that everything important is done through people, and "you must get the support of the organization. And you can only do that if they understand your objectives, if they've had an opportunity to discuss their views with you, and argue it through."

Perhaps the single most important trait these ten individuals share is their enthusiasm. As Ralph Lazarus emphasizes, enthusiasm is the key element in determining the ultimate success or failure of an idea. "Even a questionable decision carried out with passion and enthusiasm can succeed brilliantly." Dick Ferris agrees. "Whatever you do, I think it should be done with energy and commitment. And above all, with enthusiasm. And in a management position, if you can convey your enthusiasm to other people, that's half the battle. If they can see you're enthused, then they're going to feel the same way."

As I talked with each of these CEOs, I couldn't help feeling that the air around us was filled with their enthusiasm. In fact, one exceptional talent they share is the ability to generate enthusiasm in the people they deal with. Certainly, as I traveled around the country to interview these ten men, I received a "shot of enthusiasm" from each one of them—enough each time to boost my own motivation and drive for weeks on end.

These are individuals who thoroughly enjoy their work; in fact, they thrive on work. It is doubtful that they could keep up the pace they do without their enthusiasm for their jobs. As Bob Beck puts it, "You have to like what you do." He adds, "We spend so much of our time working—why not have fun at it? . . . That's what makes the day feel good." Obviously it is this attitude which enables Bob to begin his day at 6:00 A.M. and not leave his office until 6:30 P.M.—not to mention his retreat to his study at home after supper until midnight, plus an occasional weekend meeting and business trip.

Almost all these men work equally long hours—and with equal enthusiasm. Irv Shapiro arrives at Du Pont at 8:00 A.M. and leaves his office with a full briefcase at 6:00 P.M. Most weekday evenings are given over to business activity of some kind, and weekends are "study periods" when he catches up on his reading of long reports. For him, like many others, being CEO is a seven-day-a-week commitment.

"Some people marvel at the energy I put into my work," Irv admits. "What they don't understand is that this is not a job in the sense of having to go to work. It's a great experience. You live for it . . . I'd rather be here than anyplace else."

Tom Murphy, who has been at General Motors for over forty years, still maintains the same pace he has kept up from the beginning. In the office at 8:00 A.M., he leaves about 6:30 P.M. with two full briefcases. Jim Robinson arrives at his office in Manhattan's financial district about 6:45 A.M. and stays until around 7:00 P.M. He works on the way home, too. But he says of his long hours, "It's as much avocation as occupation. There really aren't very many things I'd rather be doing than what I do here."

Reg Jones similarly works a twelve-hour day, and he too credits his energy to his love of what he does. "I'm quite sure I wouldn't have the energy level or devote the amount of time I do if I wasn't enjoying it." He and other CEO's have agreed that while what they are looking for in their successors are intelligence, integrity, character, and personality, energy is vital. Reg says, "If you didn't have the high energy level, I don't know how you'd get this job done."

These men, most of them in their fifties and sixties, have higher energy levels than many people half their age. I have worked with men in their twenties with more natural stamina and in superb physical condition who were exhausted at their desks by mid-afternoon. Yet an enthusiastic CEO in his sixties can work a twelve-hour day and thrive on it. The difference seems to be their attitude toward their work—and this love of their work is also a major factor in their success.

Their enthusiasm for their jobs is coupled with a commitment to what they do. Dave Mitchell says that his work with Avon has top priority in his life. "It's hard for me to imagine someone doing this job," he says, "who didn't feel that way. . . . My job has always come first. And I think it takes that kind of total commitment to get maximum results."

This kind of commitment, Dave admits, has its price. "There's no question about it, it's detrimental to your family life. . . . I think that, like many executives, I feel guilty sometimes about not spending enough time with my family." Other CEOs also commented on the strain numerous transfers put on a growing family. During Bob Beck's first twenty years with Prudential, he and his family were transferred fourteen times. Jerry McAfee had twelve transfers at Gulf, and Charlie Brown, who has held twenty-three positions at AT&T, has probably lost count of his transfers.

Charlie believes that moving a few times can be a positive experience for a family. But, he adds, "By the fourth or fifth move, you lose a sense of roots. Instead of benefiting the family, the move can be disruptive." He points out that transfers are not as hard on the executive, who enters a familiar business environment each time he is transferred and rapidly becomes comfortable. Adjustment is more difficult for the wife and children—and sometimes not possible.

With the strain of relocations, extensive travel, and long hours on the job, a rising executive leads a life which demands a great deal of his spouse. She becomes a central factor in his success. Jerry McAfee says, "A supportive wife is about as indispensable as anything I know of. I certainly wouldn't want to try to live through my career without Geraldine's support." Dick Ferris refers to his wife, Kelsey, who moved the family ten times in ten years, as "a real trouper." "You don't have to be married to be successful," he says, "but if you are married, you have to have a supportive wife. . . . If you don't, it's like being in a horse race and carrying a forty-pound handicap."

In addition to working long hours, these CEOs give their time to community and civic activities. Unquestionably they think that their roles as influential business leaders obligate them to contribute time to society. Jim Robinson explains that he believes, as his father did, "that each of us should leave the world a little better than we found it."

For Ralph Lazarus, family comes first, business second, and community third. His strong belief that community involvement is a top priority in life has become a shared business philosophy at Federated. "We run a business that's basically a corporate citizen," Ralph explains. "We believe we should not only be generous financially, but that our people should be generous with their time, and make major commitments to the cultural, educational, and philanthropic institutions of the community."

Federated is not the only large corporation that views itself as a corporate citizen. Representing Gulf Oil at a recent annual shareholders' meeting, Jerry McAfee said, "If we are successful, it doesn't just mean that Gulf will be a bigger and stronger and more profitable company. . . . It means that the nation will have more energy resources, will be less dependent on foreign oil imports, and will enjoy a stronger economy. It also means that you will share in these rewards. . . . That's what we're working for . . . that's our goal."

Irv Shapiro points out that Du Pont encourages its people to be politically active by allowing those who hold government offices to use up to 20 percent of their working time on those activities. Irv believes that, like government, industry exists to serve the public interest and that "you cannot separate a business from the community and the nation. They are inseparable."

All ten individuals in this book are members of the Business Roundtable, which has approximately two hundred member companies. Reg Jones, the most recent co-chairman, will complete a six-year term in 1980. Irv Shapiro was chairman in 1976-77, and Tom Murphy held that post in 1978-79. CEOs who are active in the Business Roundtable or the Business Council spend a significant percentage of their time dealing with what Reg Jones calls "the externalities." The decisions made in these organizations have significant consequences in the public sector.

Today's CEOs are concerned about America's welfare, and they are willing to state their positions publicly. Often they consider their work on matters of public policy through such organizations as the Business Roundtable to be among the most significant aspects of their jobs. As Irv Shapiro states, "In the past, businessmen have been too timid about their public profiles. They've been afraid to take the heat from the press, so they've lived essentially private lives. That might have been appropriate at one time in our history, but not today. Today they have to be accessible to the media." Irv believes that the business leaders of the coming decades will follow in the footsteps of this generation of CEOs, many of whom devote a significant portion of their time to social and governmental activities.

The ten men in this book provide excellent role models for future business leaders. These are men of conscience and integrity who bear no resemblance to the stereotype of the cold-hearted business leader. On the contrary, they represent the best our society can offer. Far-seeing leaders, they seek to provide us with a better world. It is reassuring to know that big business in America is run by conscientious and capable men who are more than equal to the challenge.

About the Author

ROBERT L. SHOOK has had a successful sales career since his graduation from Ohio State University in 1959. He is chairman of the board of Shook Enterprises, author of *The Entrepreneurs, Ten Greatest Salespersons, The Real Estate People,* and *Winning Images,* and coauthor of *The Complete Professional Salesman* and *Total Commitment.* He lives in Columbus, Ohio, with his wife and three children.